The archaeology of
V. GORDON CHILDE

Frontispiece Childe lecturing at the Institute of Archaeology in St John's Lodge, wearing Central Asian dress and holding an Australian Aboriginal spear, London 1956 (from a sketch by Marjorie Maitland Howard).

The *archaeology of*
V. GORDON CHILDE
Contemporary perspectives

EDITED BY
DAVID R. HARRIS

Proceedings of the V. Gordon Childe Centennial Conference held at
the Institute of Archaeology, University College London, 8–9 May
1992 under the auspices of the Institute of Archaeology and the
Prehistoric Society.

INSTITUTE OF ARCHAEOLOGY
UNIVERSITY COLLEGE LONDON

THE PREHISTORIC SOCIETY

The University of Chicago Press

The University of Chicago Press, Chicago 60637

UCL Press Limited, University College London, London, WC1E 6BT
The name of University College London (UCL) is a registered trade mark used by UCL Press with the consent of the owner.

First published in 1994

Printed in Great Britain

03 02 01 00 99 98 97 96 95 94   1 2 3 4 5

ISBN: 0-226-31759-5 (cloth)

Library of Congress Cataloging in Publication data

V. Gordon Childe Centennial Conference (1992 : Institute of
  Archaeology, University College London)
    The archaeology of V. Gordon Childe : contemporary perspectives /
  edited by David R. Harris
      p.   cm.
    "Proceedings of the V. Gordon Childe Centennial Conference held at
  the Institute of Archaeology, University College London, 8–9 May
  1992 under the auspices of the Institute of Archaeology and the
  Prehistoric Society."
    1. Childe, V. Gordon (Vere Gordon, 1892–1957--Congresses.
    2. Archaeology--Congresses. 3. Man, Prehistoric--Congresses.
  I. Harris, David. R. (David Russell) II. Childe, V. Gordon (Vere
  Gordon), 1892–1957. III. University College London. Institute of
  Archaeology. IV. Prehistoric Society (London, England) V. Title.
  CC115.C45V2 1992
  909--dc20   93-45011
                                                                    CIP

Contents

Preface

In the Library of the London Institute of Archaeology in Gordon Square, a bronze bust of Vere Gordon Childe has gazed somewhat quizzically upon successive generations of archaeology students since shortly after the building was first occupied in 1958. What does the man, and his immense contribution to archaeology, mean to the present generation? This was the question that inspired the Childe Centennial Conference which was held at the Institute on Friday and Saturday, 8–9 May 1992. The participants came together both to celebrate the hundredth anniversary of Childe's birth and to discuss the continuing significance of his academic achievement, 35 years after he ended his life in the Blue Mountains of New South Wales, where he had spent his childhood.

The Conference was co-sponsored by the Institute of Archaeology, of which Childe was the first full-time Director, and the Prehistoric Society, of which he was the first President. My aim in organizing the meeting was to invite a small group of internationally distinguished prehistorians to examine different aspects of Childe's scholarship and to assess the relevance of his work to archaeology in the 1990s. Ample time was to be allowed for discussion, and it was hoped that the outcome would warrant publication of the proceedings. Happily, this hope proved fully justified, for the Conference was a remarkable academic event – notable for the quality and originality of the speakers' papers, the vigour and humour of the discussions, and the general atmosphere of celebration. The presence of some of Childe's former colleagues and students added greatly to the occasion, and among the 100 or so participants were two past Presidents of the Prehistoric Society: Professor Sir Grahame Clark and Professor John Evans (Figs 1, 2).

On the Friday morning Professor Bruce Trigger of McGill University got the Conference off to an impressive start with a paper that examined the range and creativity, as well as the limitations, of Childe's thought, arguing that Childe had contributed not only to culture-historical and evolutionary archaeology but had also in some ways anticipated the more recent ideas of processual and post-processual archaeologists. Professor Michael Rowlands of University College London then explored the ethical and moral imperatives of Childe's work and their roots in 18th- and 19th-century European philosophy, and suggested that Childe had concocted "a grand sociological history of freedom". This original intellectual excursion was followed by a contrasting paper by Professor John Mulvaney of the Australian Academy of the Humanities, which revealed a new and surprising perspective on Childe. He posed the question of what "invisible (intellectual and psychological) baggage" Childe brought with him when he left Australia for Britain in 1921, and described how the Australian Intelligence Service persistently interfered with Childe's attempts to fund academic employment in New South Wales and Queensland – a revelation that gives new meaning to Childe's statement that he "would have chosen revolutionary politics but the price was too high".

On the Friday evening there was a reception at the Institute followed by a Conference Dinner at UCL at which we were entertained, and moved, by the vivid memories of some of those present who had known Childe, including Sinclair Hood, Nancy Sandars, Jay Butler and Peter Gathercole. They recalled his essential kindliness as well as his eccentricities. Other amusing and revealing memories of Childe were sent to me by some of his former students who were unable to attend the Conference, and three of these – from Charles Thomas, Frank Mitchell and Howard Kilbride-Jones – are included in this volume as a Postscript (pp. 135–40).

More revelations were to follow on the Saturday. On his first visit to Britain, Professor Leo Klejn of the Russian Academy of Sciences in St Petersburg, whom I had invited to speak on "Childe's relations with Soviet archaeology", delivered an academic bombshell. With grace and wit, he likened Childe's affair with Soviet archaeology to a knight's romance, which, although based on mutual love, could not end happily. That it did not was made dramatically clear when Professor Klejn produced a letter, previously unknown in the West, that Childe wrote in December 1956, ten months before his death, to a group of prominent Soviet archaeologists. In it he criticized, directly and in detail, the objectives and methods of his Soviet colleagues. A facsimile of the letter is included in this volume (pp. 94–100).

These Russian revelations were followed by a new insight into Childe's influence – or lack of it – on American archaeology offered by Professor Kent Flannery of the University of Michigan. In an incisive analysis he examined Childe's famous models of the Neolithic and Urban Revolutions in relation to the rich archaeological record from "Nuclear America" and concluded that Childe "tended consistently to underrate [the] level of development of . . . New World cultures".

The Conference was rounded off skilfully by Professor Colin Renfrew of the University of Cambridge. He touched on some of the main points raised by earlier speakers and went on to argue persuasively that Childe "might well be regarded as a processualist". However, ultimately, "he was not a 'new' archaeologist" and remained "a particularist . . . because he did not really embrace the possibilities for generalization offered by his own work".

In two exciting and memorable days, new and unexpected light was shed on Childe the archaeologist and the man – a man who was both of his time and ahead of his time. The success of the Conference was due not only to the excellence of the speakers' papers but also to the quality of the discussions, edited versions of which have been included to give the full flavour of the occasion. I offer my warm thanks to all those who participated, including colleagues who kindly chaired individual sessions – John Wilkes, Roy Hodson, Peter Gathercole and Stephen Shennan – as well as the students who assisted so willingly with the organization; Belinda Barratt, the Institute's Librarian, and Elaine Sansom, our Lecturer in Museum Studies, who assembled a display for the Conference from the Institute's Childe archive; and especially Katherine Wright of the Institute's Department of Western Asiatic Archaeology and Mary Moloney, my Assistant, who calmly carried most of the organizational burden before and during the meeting. Mary, too, gave unstinting assistance in the preparation of the text for publication.

If this book conveys the spirit as well as the content of what was a remarkable conference, and helps to bring Childe's achievements into fresh focus for present and future archaeologists, it will have achieved its aims.

DAVID R. HARRIS

List of illustrations

Frontispiece Childe lecturing at the Institute of Archaeology in St John's Lodge, wearing Central Asian dress and holding an Australian Aboriginal spear, London 1956 (from a sketch by Marjorie Maitland Howard).

Plates (between pages 68 and 69)

1a David Harris opening the Conference on 8 May 1992.
1b Conference speakers, chairmen, and former colleagues and students of Childe on the steps of the Institute, Gordon Square, London, 8 May 1992.
2a Childe at Skara Brae, Orkney, 1929.
2b Childe at the entrance to the Museu de Sanfins, northern Portugal, December 1949.
3a Childe, Grahame Clark and others on a Prehistoric Society visit to Dartmoor, September 1949.
3b Childe "in the field" during a Prehistoric Society Study Tour to Cumbria, September 1948.
3c Childe at the site of Ruse, Bulgaria, April 1955.
3d Childe at Kazanluk, Bulgaria, April 1995.
4a Childe in his room at the Institute of Archaeology, St John's Lodge, Regent's Park, London.
4b The Institute's staff outside St John's Lodge in 1955.

Footnote: The Frontispiece and the photographs reproduced as Plates 1a, 1b, 3c, 3d, 4a and 4b are from the Childe archive in the Library of the Institute of Archaeology. Those reproduced as Plates 2b, 3a and 3b were kindly donated to the Prehistoric Society in June 1993 by Marion Jennings, were taken by her and others, and copies are now in the Childe archive at the Institute. Plate 2a is reproduced by courtesy of the Orkney Library Photographic Archive, and thanks are due to Peter Gathercole for drawing the editor's attention to it. The Frontispiece and Plate 4b were published previously, in J. D. Evans, "The first half-century – and after", *Bulletin of the Institute of Archaeology, University College London* 24 (1987), 1-25.

List of contributors

V. Gordon Childe Abercromby Professor of Archaeology,
(1892–1957)   University of Edinburgh, 1927–46
Director, and Professor of Prehistoric European
Archaeology, Institute of Archaeology,
University of London, 1946–56
President of the Prehistoric Society, 1935–36

Kent V. Flannery Professor of Anthropology and Curator of Archaeology,
University of Michigan

David R. Harris Director, and Professor of Human Environment,
Institute of Archaeology, University College London
President of the Prehistoric Society, 1990–94

Leo S. Klejn Professor of Archaeology, Russian Asoociation of
Scientists, St Petersburg

John Mulvaney Secretary, Australian Academy of the Humanities
Emeritus Professor of Prehistory, Australian National
University

Colin Renfrew Disney Professor of Archaeology, University of
Cambridge

Michael Rowlands Professor of Anthropology, University College London

Bruce G. Trigger Professor of Anthropology, McGill University

Introduction

DAVID R. HARRIS

There can be few if any archaeologists in the world, old or young, who have not heard of, and probably read something by, Vere Gordon Childe. In Bruce Trigger's words, in the opening paragraph of his paper in this volume: "Childe, although dead since 1957, remains the most renowned and widely read archaeologist of the 20th century". Why should this be so? That is, in essence, the question that inspired all the participants in the conference which gave rise to this book. The meeting was in part a celebration of Childe's life and extraordinary scholarly achievement, but its primary purpose was to examine the continuing significance of his work a century after his birth.

This book is not intended as a contribution to the history of archaeology, although there is much in it to interest an historian of the subject. Nor is its aim biographical, although it is neither possible nor desirable to separate the man from his ideas. Relevant and revealing biographical details are to be found in it, particularly in John Mulvaney's and Leo Klejn's contributions, and they add materially to our understanding of Childe's intellectual development. But the main agenda of the conference was to review Childe's achievement from different – partly national – perspectives and to assess how far, and why, it remains significant for today's students of the human past.

For the older participants, some of whom had personal memories of the man, Childe was himself an inseparable part of our own perception of the past. For the generation who came archaeologically of age before the 1960s, he personified – indeed largely created – the emerging discipline of prehistory. He was the scholar who for the first time *made sense* of the prehistoric past of Europe as a whole, and, by extension, of the Near East (Southwest Asia). At a time when European archaeologists were preoccupied with regional sites and sequences, it was he who had the vision, the knowledge and the skill to construct the first prehistory of the whole continent (1925) and the first ordered and comprehensive account of the ancient Near East (1928).

Few 20th-century archaeologists have failed to be influenced by the interpretive framework that Childe built, and revised, in *The dawn of European civilization* and *The most ancient East* in their original and successive editions. Even if some later reactions to his Eurocentric, diffusionist model of the past were highly critical (e.g. Renfrew 1973, and, at a greater spatial remove, Harris 1972), and others were impeded by political barriers (cf. Klejn's refer-

1

ence in this volume to the long-delayed translation of *The dawn* into Russian), few if any interpretations of the prehistoric past, in or beyond Europe, were unaffected by the mental template that Childe had constructed. His influence was felt least in North America (cf. Flannery in this volume), but even there, for example, the adoption of maize-based agriculture north of Mexico was often ascribed to a process of diffusion from the south broadly comparable to Childe's model for the spread of agriculture from the (subtropical) Near East to and through (temperate) Europe (e.g. Caldwell 1962, Haury 1962).

Childe's extraordinary ability to read, retain and relate archaeological evidence in many languages referring to myriad sites, and to synthesize the results, has often been applauded. Kent Flannery puts it more succinctly at the end of his contribution to this volume: Childe, he says, was "the man who made order out of archaeological chaos". One of the questions asked at the conference was whether the order he created, in the prehistory of Europe and the Near East, was still valid. It is not surprising that, over half a century later, and armed with the powerful comparative method of radiocarbon dating, most of his chronological and spatial interpretations have been rejected or substantially revised. This point was emphasized a decade ago by Ruth Tringham:

> Gordon Childe was seen as a great synthesizer of data; but now that the data have outgrown his syntheses, they have been superseded. His interpretational models have been regarded as either refuted or untest-able. V. Gordon Childe and his works have been relegated to the history of the discipline and, as such, are generally regarded as irrelevant to current developments in research into the evolution of culture and society. (Tringham 1983: 87)

Trigger makes the same point in this volume, adding that Childe himself foresaw the rejection of his own interpretations (Childe 1958: 74); and he then goes on to state what can be regarded as the central theme – and even conclusion – of the conference: that, despite the rejection of his interpretational models, Childe's "theoretical work continues to inspire and to resonate with the perspectives of successive generations of archaeologists and with new fashions of archaeological interpretation". That, essentially, is why Childe's ideas remain relevant in the 1990s and why his work transcends the prime place it undoubtedly occupies in the history of archaeology.

What then does Childe's "theoretical work" comprise and how does it relate to contemporary perspectives in archaeology? Aspects of this very large question were discussed at the conference and are addressed explicitly or implicitly in most of the papers. They can be construed as falling into three simplified and not mutually exclusive categories concerning (a) the nature of cultures and the rôle of culture history; (b) cultural evolution; and (c) Marxist interpretations of history.

Bruce Trigger and Colin Renfrew both stress the enduring importance in Childe's intellectual life of his first venture as a young man into archaeology:

2

his interest in the origin of the Greeks which in turn led to the larger ambition of identifying archaeologically the earliest Indo-Europeans. The influences of his teachers in classics, philosophy, ancient history and archaeology at the universities of Sydney and Oxford are alluded to, respectively, by John Mulvaney and Colin Renfrew, and Bruce Trigger suggests that this early interest underlies his lifetime's desire to account for the origins of what he saw as the distinctiveness and greatness of European civilization. There is indeed an impressive symmetry in a scholarly career in which the first and final books – separated by 33 years and over 250 other publications on a vast range of topics – focus on the same theme (Childe 1925, 1958).

It was in *The dawn of European civilization* (1925) that Childe first used the culture-historical approach combined with the principle of diffusion in what was to become the prevailing mode of archaeological interpretation in the West – until the new archaeology burst upon the scene in the 1960s. Childe defined archaeological cultures in terms of distinctive assemblages of material traits and criticized those who labelled every local variety of pottery a new "culture", a definition which he still espoused at the end of his life (see, in this volume, the final paragraph of the letter he wrote to Soviet colleagues in December 1956). He was careful, however, to avoid crude assumptions of equivalence between "cultures" and "peoples", and he sought to distinguish between persistent traits, such as burial customs, which were likely to be associated with particular ethnic groups for long periods of time, and more transient or widespread traits, such as new tools or weapons, which, he argued, would tend to spread relatively rapidly from one group to another.

Despite this discriminating approach to the evidence of "cultures" in the archaeological record, Childe continued to try to trace historically known peoples back into the European prehistoric past, becoming ever more sceptical about the possibility of doing so. In this sense, as Renfrew argues in this volume, he remained a particularist, unwilling to develop cross-cultural comparisons and generalizations about processes of socioeconomic change, while, incidentally, also largely ignoring ethnographic evidence. But, although he entirely avoided the racist excesses of some of his contemporaries, notably Gustaf Kossinna, he could not completely shed a belief in the innate differences of ethnic groups. This is what both Rowlands and Renfrew refer to in this volume as Childe's "essentialism". Although, as Renfrew aptly expresses it: "it seemed in some way to matter [to Childe] which 'peoples' were which", he did not subscribe to any notion of ethnic purity. On the contrary, he frequently appealed to the concept of ethnic mixing as an invigorating, culturally dynamic process which led to "progress".

It is this aspect of Childe's thinking on cultures and cultural history that Mike Rowlands focuses upon in his exploration of the intellectual background, in the 18th and 19th centuries, of Childe's ethical position; and he uses Childe's advocacy of the importance of cultural mixing as a platform from which to launch his own examination of the processes of cultural "hybridization", particularly in relation to the rôle of Creole and pidgin languages in linguistic history – a currently controversial question that is further debated in the discussion that follows Rowlands's paper.

The second main theme in Childe's theoretical work that can be identified concerns his contributions to the study of cultural evolution. Here we arrive at what to many archaeologists remain Childe's most original and widely applicable generalizations about the human past: his concepts of the Neolithic and Urban Revolutions. These theoretical models were first proposed in *New light on the most ancient East* (1934), and, in the case of the Urban Revolution, fully elaborated in Childe's famous paper of that name in *The Town Planning Review* (1950).

In his incisive and illuminating contribution to this volume, Kent Flannery exposes these formative models to the rich – and, in the case of chiefdom societies, even "flamboyant" – New World archaeological record, and finds the fit between the models and the data far from close. This is not surprising considering the vast amount of well directed research that has taken place in "Nuclear America" since 1950, and considering the well known fact that Childe showed little interest in, and paid only superficial attention to, the evidence for native American civilizations (not excepting reference to the Maya in his 1950 paper). But the continuing influence of Childe's "revolutions" on archaeological interpretation is neatly exemplified in Flannery's paper, in which he argues that, at least for Nuclear America, a third revolution needs to be interposed between the Neolithic and the Urban (the "Rank Revolution") and that warfare should be substituted for writing in Childe's ten criteria for urban civilization. These revisions are offered both as criticism and commendation of Childe's formulations, and Flannery encapsulates their enduring value in his concluding statement:

> It hardly matters that some details of Childe's scheme don't fit the current Nuclear American data. What matters is that Childe had a vision of evolution at a time when other archaeologists had only chronology charts.

But we can properly ask: how far did Childe's "vision of evolution" extend? In his paper, Trigger points out that in the late 1920s and early 1930s Childe was already doubting the value of an ethnically based culture–historical approach and had begun to focus on more general economic and technical changes, in themselves and as a means of understanding other cultural changes. This soon led him to the idea of successive revolutions as engines of demographic, social and political transformations which were essentially irreversible. "Progress" was achieved through human effort and inventiveness; it was not determined by external forces. Thus, although Childe was becoming a proponent of functionalism, he was not an environmental or ecological determinist. Even in his model of the Neolithic Revolution in the Near East, in which increasing desiccation is treated as a "prime mover", it is by deliberate human intervention that plants and animal are domesticated (although precisely *how* this might have occurred he never discusses).

Childe's early interest in major economic and technical innovations (domestication, the beginnings of metallurgy, urbanism), as well as his less well know pioneering work on settlement forms and functions, particularly in Scotland (discussed by Trigger in this volume), have led to the suggestion that he was a forerunner of the "processual" archaeologists of the 1960s and 1970s. Renfrew argues cogently in this volume that Childe was "in several ways a pioneer of processual archaeology" but concludes that there is a paradox "in Childe's life of many paradoxes" between his rôle "as a processual or 'new archaeologist', very much heralding the archaeology of the 1960s and 1970s, and Childe as a traditional, historical archaeologist, preferring narrative to analysis".

In speculating on how far Childe's thinking, from the 1930s onwards, was evolutionary, or in some senses even processual, we approach what is a very fine distinction between his rôle as an evolutionist and as a Marxist interpreter of history. In this volume Trigger, Rowlands and Renfrew all stress the significance of Childe's emphasis – within an overall evolutionary framework – on human cultures as *social* constructs rather than as products only of their environmental and technological contexts. This assertion of the importance of human action in shaping society was, as Renfrew notes, most aptly expressed by Childe in the title of *Man makes himself* (1936), and it becomes even more explicit later in *Social evolution* (1951). This view is of course an integral part of Marxist philosophy, and Childe's espousal of it may partly account for his relative disregard of environmental and ecological factors in cultural history.

Childe's commitment to Marxism as a philosophical system increased during the 1930s, particularly after his first visit to the Soviet Union in 1935, but there is very little evidence of this in his academic archaeological publications. Indeed, as Klejn shows, in his highly original contribution, Childe was at first perceived by most of his archaeological colleagues in the Soviet Union as a "dangerous Marxist".

It was not until Stalinist intellectual orthodoxies began to be eroded in the postwar period that translations of some of Childe's major works into Russian began to appear: *The dawn* in 1952 and *New light on the most ancient East* in 1954. And we now know that he remained highly critical of Soviet archaeology to the end of his life. This was dramatically demonstrated at the conference when Klejn revealed the existence of a letter, previously unknown in the West and reproduced in facsimile in this volume, which Childe wrote to unnamed archaeological colleagues in the Soviet Union in December 1956, less than a year before his suicide in Australia in October 1957. It is perhaps surprising that the letter is concerned almost entirely with criticisms of Soviet archaeological *practice* rather than theory, and that Childe's sceptical attitude to Marxist interpretations of prehistory in terms of unilinear evolution remains unexpressed. This point was raised by Barbara Bender in discussion after Klejn's paper, and Klejn has since suggested that one of the reasons for the absence of any reference to theory may have been that Childe preferred to avoid further antagonizing colleagues whom he regarded as friends and with whom to engage in theoretical argument would have been in vain.

Trigger argues (in this volume) that as Childe became progressively disillusioned with Soviet archaeology through the 1940s and 1950s he turned more to Marxism as a philosophical system. He began to take a more sophisticated view of human behaviour, for example by acknowledging the rôle of perception as an intermediary between individuals and their social and natural environments, although he remained a materialist and rationalist who asserted that archaeologists could, by learning more about how cultures developed in the past, contribute to the "science of progress".

The papers in this book reflect and explore many facets of Childe's life, ideas and achievements. They do not pretend to offer a carefully constructed critique of his prodigious contribution to archaeology, nor an assessment of how his life affected his work, although both those themes recur in the pages that follow. The book is partly celebratory, as was the conference it reports, but its aim is mainly to demonstrate the dynamic qualities of Childe's thought, the breadth and depth of his scholarship, and the continuing relevance of much of his work to contemporary issues in archaeology. While the debate between "processualists" and "post-processualists" continues, it is salutary to be reminded of how close Childe came to a holistic vision of archaeology as a social science, without losing confidence in the ability of archaeologists to "piece together the past" and contribute their knowledge to the making of a better future. In these ecologically, economically and politically troubled times, Childe's attachment to the idea of progress may seem naïve, but in *la longue durée* of prehistory it need not seem absurd. Let him, therefore, have the last (optimistic) word, in fact the last sentence of what, as Trigger suggests, is probably the most widely read book ever written by an archaeologist, *What happened in history*:

> Progress is real if discontinuous. The upward curve resolves itself into a series of troughs and crests. But in those domains that archaeology as well as history can survey, no trough ever declines to the low level of the preceding one, each crest out-tops its last precursor.

References

Caldwell, J. R. 1962. Eastern North America. In *Courses toward urban life*, R. J. Braidwood & G. R. Willey (eds), 288–308. Chicago: Aldine.

Childe, V. G. 1925. *The dawn of European civilization*. London: Kegan Paul, Trench, Trubner.

1928. *The most ancient East: the oriental prelude to European prehistory*. London: Kegan Paul, Trench, Trubner.

1934. *New light on the most ancient East: the oriental prelude to European prehistory*. London: Kegan Paul, Trench, Trubner.

1936. *Man makes himself.* London: Watts.

1950. The urban revolution. *The Town Planning Review* 21, 3–17.

1951. *Social evolution.* London: Watts.

1958. *The prehistory of European society.* Harmondsworth: Penguin.

Harris, D. R. 1972. The origins of agriculture in the tropics. *American Scientist* 60, 180–93.

Haury, E. W. 1962. The greater American Southwest. In *Courses toward urban life,* R. J. Braidwood & G. R. Willey (eds), 106–31. Chicago: Aldine.

Renfrew, A. C. 1973. *Before civilization: the radiocarbon revolution and prehistoric Europe.* London: Cape.

Tringham, R. 1983. V. Gordon Childe 25 years after; his relevance for the archaeology of the eighties. *Journal of Field Archaeology* 10, 85–100.

Childe's relevance to the 1990s

BRUCE G. TRIGGER

Prehistory is still a dialogue with the ghost of Childe
Andrew Sherratt 1989: 185

Vere Gordon Childe, although dead since 1957, remains the most renowned and widely read archaeologist of the 20th century. Already during his lifetime his books were translated into many languages and his accomplishments were honoured by colleagues around the world. The range of his interests was prodigious, producing in the eyes of his contemporaries not one but several different Childes. Most European archaeologists recognized him as the leading expert on the culture-history of prehistoric Europe. In the United States, he was acknowledged to be one of the foremost cultural evolutionists of his time, while in Latin America he became the primary exponent of a Marxist approach to archaeology. Few of his contemporaries seem to have been fully aware of the diversity of his interests and of his publications. Childe's was an extraordinary achievement, especially since he became an archaeologist relatively late in life and his major works were published over a span of only 32 years.

There was also considerable disagreement during his lifetime about what Childe really believed. In his interactions with colleagues he kept his personal feelings to himself, and one senses even in his correspondence with friends and relatives a desire to appear the sort of person that he thought each of them wanted him to be. This was probably the behaviour of a man who was shy and insecure in his personal life. He also tended to mute theoretical disagreements with people whose company he valued, especially members of left-wing political groups, a trait which may have inhibited his critical thinking about various archaeological problems. Yet he enjoyed shocking his more conservative associates. His concern that a copy of the *Daily Worker* should be clearly visible in his office and his tongue-in-cheek delight in imitating Soviet praises of "Comrade Stalin" are well known. Sally Green (1981: 77) has shrewdly suggested that much of this behaviour was "a form of protection", based on the correct assumption that conservative scholars might accept him more readily if he made it possible for them to laugh off his Communist tendencies. As a result, he convinced some of his colleagues that his professed Marxism was an elaborate hoax. It is therefore not surprising that, when he died, his contemporaries found themselves far from agreed about the nature and significance of his accomplishments.

9

Childe's heritage

Thirty-five years after his death, Childe remains an enigma. Although he was the leading expert of his generation on the prehistory of Europe, his interpretations of that prehistory have largely been rejected, as he foresaw they would be (Childe 1958a: 74; Sherratt 1989). Yet his theoretical work continues to inspire and to resonate with the perspectives of successive generations of archaeologists and with new fashions of archaeological interpretation. The economic and settlement studies that he pioneered in the 1930s and 1940s have much in common with the processual or social archaeology of the 1960s and 1970s. His philosophical writings, which attracted little attention during his lifetime, have acquired increasing significance in the context of the post-processual archaeology that developed in the 1980s, while in Europe and North America a new generation of Marxist archaeologists, who were little impressed by the orthodoxies of Soviet archaeology, found in these works both inspiration (Leone 1972: 12; Spriggs 1977: 5–9; Kohl 1984) and much to disagree with (Kus 1983: 279–83; 1984: 103–104; Gathercole 1984: 152). Childe has also been subjected in recent years to bitter attacks by those who continue to be repelled by his espousal of Marxism and the cordial relations he appeared to have with Soviet archaeologists (Clark 1976).

Three decades after their deaths, the ideas of most scholars are of little more than historical interest. It is an extraordinary testimonial to the vigour of Childe's scholarship that many of his writings still inspire controversy and debate and that, in an age that has a compulsive desire to debunk outstanding individuals, successive generations of archaeologists continue to discover significant features in his work that had not been obvious previously. Intellectual developments during the past decade have emphasized important aspects of his work that I had thought to be of little significance when I studied his writings in the 1970s. I conclude that, in at least some respects, Childe was an archaeologist well ahead of his time.

Childe is not an ideal subject for even an intellectual biography. He destroyed most of his papers and correspondence when he retired. His notebooks, while voluminous and in some respects informative, do not answer as many questions about the development of his thinking as might be expected. Most of what we know about Childe comes from his published works. These reveal that, while his interests continued to expand throughout his career and his interpretations of archaeological data altered radically over time, only rarely did he totally repudiate his older ideas. In spite of this, it is clear that the general views that guided his work in the 1950s were very different from those that had guided it in the 1920s, or in the 1930s and 1940s. Each successive phase in the development of his thinking made a significant original contribution to the archaeology of his day. The purpose of this paper is to consider the significance for modern archaeology of the various stages in the development of his thought.

Culture–historical archaeology

Childe began as a classics student at the University of Sydney. His first ambition was to discover the homeland of the Indo-European speaking peoples
and, in order to do this, like the German linguist Gustaf Kossinna, he turned
to archaeological evidence. Childe was more successful than most archaeologists of the 1920s in avoiding the racism that permeated the social sciences
at that period (Childe 1926). Yet his research was characterized throughout
his career by a desire to account for the origins of what he saw as the
distinctiveness and greatness of European civilization during the historical
period. In his earliest works he followed his mentors, John L. Myres and
Arthur Evans, in attributing that greatness to the manner in which technological innovations of Near Eastern origin had been put to new social uses as
a result of the political genius and dynamism of nomadic Indo-European
conquerors who had supposedly entered Europe from the steppes of Central
Asia.

In 1925 Childe combined the diffusionism of Oscar Montelius with Gustaf
Kossinna's concept of prehistory as a mosaic of archaeological cultures to
produce *The dawn of European civilization*. In this book he rejected Kossinna's
racism, which attributed all human progress to the biological superiority of
an Indo-European master race. This was also the first book to try to treat the
prehistory of the whole of Europe during the Neolithic and Bronze ages not
as a mere chronicle of technological development but as a history of different
peoples and their changing ways of life. *The dawn of European civilization*
provided a model for the culture–historical approach to European prehistory
that was to dominate archaeological interpretation around the world for the
next three decades (Rouse 1972).

The basis of Childe's approach was his definition of archaeological cultures,
which was done in terms of artifact types; an operation aided by Childe's
extensive reading knowledge of European languages and his keen visual memory. By adopting a culture–historical approach, he was better able to account
for geographical variations in the archaeological record than earlier generations of evolutionary archaeologists, or straightforward diffusionists such as
Montelius, had done. By showing how technologies of Near Eastern origin
had been adopted by various peoples living in different sorts of environments,
Childe demonstrated that the development of culture in prehistoric Europe
had required innovation at the local as well as at the regional and pan-human
levels.

While Childe mostly constructed his culture–historical approach out of
ideas that were already present in archaeology, he made original contributions
that foreshadowed later developments in his thinking. In some of his later
writings, perhaps under the influence of American Boasian anthropologists, he
offered purely normative definitions of the concept of the archaeological
culture as being a complex of regularly associated traits which represented the

way of life of a particular people. This has led Lewis Binford and Jeremy Sabloff (1982) to dismiss Childe as yet another early 20th-century archaeologist who viewed cultures as collections of homogeneously shared and hence diagnostically equivalent traits. As early as 1929, however, Childe distinguished between traits that had functioned as ethnic indicators and ones that were primarily of technological significance. He argued that the former, which included hand-made pottery and burial customs, tended to persist relatively unchanged for long periods among particular peoples and hence could provide evidence of ethnic identity. On the other hand, new and more efficient tools and weapons were likely to have diffused quickly from one group to another, since considerable advantages could be derived from utilizing them (Childe 1929: vii, 248).

Childe believed that both sorts of evidence were necessary for a culture–historical analysis. Ethnically persistent traits permitted peoples to be identified and traced in the archaeological record; functionally efficient ones, because they diffused rapidly from one culture to another, allowed contemporary cultures to be temporally correlated. In this fashion, he believed that it was possible to fit archaeological cultures into spatial and temporal frameworks, which revealed not only technological change but also how different groups of peoples had moved around Europe in prehistoric times. While Childe decided which traits were ethnically and technologically significant on the basis of common sense rather than ethnological studies, he was one of the first archaeologists to introduce explicitly functional considerations into the study of archaeological data.

Childe gradually abandoned the search for an Indo-European homeland as something that could never be determined for certain on the basis of archaeological evidence (Childe 1930: 240–47; 1958a: 69; 1958b: 2). Yet for the rest of his life his research continued to focus on European and Near Eastern prehistory. In the course of the 1930s, he ascribed positive moral and political value to diffusionism because it revealed the errors of Nazi racism. Childe believed that diffusionism ascribed to peoples from all parts of the world an active rôle in the creation of a universal cultural heritage. He stressed, for example, how humanity as a whole had benefited in recent centuries from the worldwide diffusion of cultigens that had been developed by many different peoples and races (Childe 1933a, b; 1942a: 16–17).

Yet, despite Childe's theoretical concern with cultures around the world, he exhibited little interest in non-European archaeological sequences. He noted, late in his career, that the Maya had created a brilliant civilization in Mesoamerica although they had not possessed any metal tools, and he acknowledged that this had important implications for understanding the development of all civilizations (Childe 1951: 26–7). Yet even his later interest in cultural evolution did not induce him to pay significant attention to cultures other than those of Europe and the Near East. Like the rationalists of the 18th century, Childe acknowledged the existence of non-Western civilizations but treated them as tributaries that were destined to join the main stream of European civilization as the latter expanded to embrace all humanity (Childe 1942a: 16–7). His lack of any serious comparative interest in cultures is as noteworthy as his continuing loyalty to the concept of diffusion as the principal creative force in human history.

Yet, in fairness to Childe, we must note that before the 1960s, few other archaeologists had more than a regional interest in prehistory. Only after that time did a growing battery of radiocarbon dates make it possible to correlate regional sequences of development on a worldwide basis and to compare rates as well as sequences of change in prehistoric times. This new perspective found expression in the work of Grahame Clark. In the 1940s and 1950s, Clark had pioneered the economic study of the past, especially the interpretation of subsistence data, and had sought new ways to recover information about human behaviour through excavation and the analysis of archaeological data (Clark 1939; 1952; 1954). Because Clark's interpretations were based largely on generalizations about plants, animals, and technology, they could be applied to all prehistoric societies.

Throughout his career, Childe remained a geographical possibilist, who believed that the natural environment limits but does not determine the nature of individual cultures. As a result, he did not contribute to the theoretical development of an ecologically orientated archaeology nearly as much as did the American anthropologist Julian Steward (1955) and archaeologist Lewis Binford (1962), who believed that ecological factors played a major rôle in the development of culture, or Clark, who maintained pragmatically, like many other archaeologists of the 1950s, that ecological factors were the most susceptible to archaeological investigation. Hence it is not surprising that it was Clark's *World prehistory: an outline* (1961), published four years after Childe's death, that pioneered a world view of prehistory. Its perspectives on cultural development prefigured the ecologism and neo-evolutionism that would characterize the New Archaeology and anticipated the beginning of the new era of processual archaeology.

The widespread evidence of slower rates of cultural change than had hitherto been imagined, which resulted from radiocarbon dating, and the growing evidence of largely autonomous sequences of cultural development in different parts of the world, called into question the value of diffusionism as an explanation of cultural change. Calibrated radiocarbon dates provided the basis for Renfrew's (1973a) revisionist interpretation of European prehistory, which stressed the creativity of prehistoric Europeans and the independence of European cultural development from that found in the Near East. Renfrew thus encouraged an internalist understanding of technological change that transcended anything that Childe had attempted, and provided the basis for the detailed and multifaceted studies that have more recently characterized the investigation of European prehistory (Renfrew 1972, Bradley 1984, Wells 1984, Whittle 1985, Chapman 1990, Hodder 1990). Renfrew also demonstrated that many of the "facts" which had been assumed to support the diffusionist interpretation of European prehistory were themselves products of diffusionist assumptions. The short chronology, which had appeared to exclude the possibility of there having been enough time for major internal changes to have occurred in the course of European prehistory, turned out to be an erroneous interpretation that had been constructed in accordance with diffusionist principles (see also Sherratt 1989: 181). Today, although diffusion (often under other names) is once again considered to provide an acceptable explanation for certain aspects of cultural change that have taken place in the course of European prehistory (Renfrew & Shennan 1982, Rowlands et al. 1987), it does so only as part of a more complex and sophisticated theoretical framework.

Functionalist approaches

Childe continued to produce revised versions of *The dawn of European civilization* for the rest of the his life, as well as more detailed culture–historical syntheses of the prehistory of the Danube Valley (1929), the Near East (1928, 1934), Scotland (1935), and England (1940). Yet, soon after he had published the first edition of *The dawn of European civilization*, he began to express serious reservations about whether such studies had significant value. Childe increasingly doubted that there was a sufficient correlation between ethnicity and material culture for archaeologists to be able to trace historically known peoples far back into the past, a position that accorded with that held by Boasian anthropologists in the United States. He also concluded that, in any case, ethnic studies were nothing more than the archaeological equivalent of an antiquated political history (Childe 1930: 240–7; 1958a: 70).

As a replacement for his culture–historical approach, Childe undertook a series of studies of economic developments in prehistoric times. In rapid succession, he examined the impacts of plant and animal domestication and of metallurgy in the Near East and Europe (Childe 1928, 1930). In *New light on the most ancient East* (1934), he construed these impacts as revolutions which, like the Industrial Revolution, had irreversibly transformed human history.

Childe's interpretations often were based on very little archaeological data. He assumed that all three revolutions had many features in common, which led him to postulate tenuous and often misleading parallels between the Industrial Revolution and earlier episodes of cultural change. He imagined that Sumerian cities had supported their populations by being major centres of industrial production and that each successive revolution had been followed by a major increase in population (Childe 1934: 42, 285–8). Yet, despite such defects, these studies demonstrated, better than any previous ones had done, the importance of investigating technological and economic changes in prehistoric times as a basis for understanding other forms of change. Childe was neither an ecological determinist nor a unilinear evolutionist. Yet he began at this time to look for explanations of regularities in the history of Europe and the Near East which most other culture–historical archaeologists had either ignored or been content to attribute to diffusion. Just as Childe's culture–historical approach had added a geographical dimension to previous evolutionary concerns with change over time, so his growing functionalism added a further social dimension to the culture–historical approach.

Until 1935, Childe, like most other Western archaeologists, attributed technological change to human beings consciously applying their powers of inventiveness to control nature more effectively and make their lives easier and more secure, an idea derived from the Enlightenment. His first direct contacts with Soviet archaeologists in 1935 convinced him that technological change had to be understood in a social and political context which was able both to promote and to retard the process of innovation and the willingness of societies to accept new ideas. This encouraged him to search for ways in which specific instances of social and political behaviour, as well as religious beliefs, could be inferred from the archaeological record.

Already in 1931, Childe had published an account of the excavations at the settlement of Skara Brae in the Orkney Islands. The furnishings of these houses had been largely constructed of stone slabs and had therefore survived in the archaeological record. Childe interpreted these remains in terms of what was known about the social organization of traditional rural houses in the Scottish Highlands and the Hebrides during the 19th century. In these houses, women and children tended to work and sleep on one side of the house and men on the other. While Skara Brae has turned out to be considerably older than Childe had imagined, his study was one of the first to apply gender principles relating to the use of space to the interpretation of archaeological data. It also illustrates Childe's early and lasting belief in the greater efficacy of analogues based on assumptions of cultural continuity than of behavioural generalizations derived from cross-cultural comparisons.

In 1940, Childe (1942b) carried out a survey of megalithic monuments on the island of Rousay, correlating their distribution with that of arable land and attempting to use the number of these monuments to estimate the size of the Neolithic population of the island. This was one of the first employments of archaeological survey as a source of information about the past rather than simply as a means of locating sites for excavation. He also suggested that, where settlements are known to have been occupied simultaneously, a line drawn half way between them would indicate the size of their respective territories (Childe 1951: 56). In the 1940s, Childe collected information about variations in the size of Neolithic settlements throughout Europe, noting that they rarely exceeded a few hundred inhabitants (Childe 1950: 5). He did not, however, draw any behavioral conclusions from this observation.

From Soviet archaeologists, Childe also adopted the idea that cemeteries could be major sources of information about social change in prehistoric times. In *Scotland before the Scots* (1946a), he interpreted the change from collective to individual burials in Neolithic and Bronze Age times as evidence for the transformation of egalitarian societies based on the collective ownership of resources into more hierarchical ones based on the private ownership of land and herds. Childe also concluded that, at an early stage in the development of states, rulers expressed their power by means of lavish burials involving the interment of many of their personal possessions. Later, as these states became more consolidated, the "greed of heirs" curtailed this lavish consumption of riches, and upper-class burials became more modest (Childe 1945). Childe based this hypothesis on interpretations that the Soviet archaeologists A. P. Kruglov and G. V. Podgayetskij (1935) had published of prehistoric burial sequences in the Ukraine, but he supported it with archaeological data concerning trends in high-status burials from many parts of the world. This study constitutes an important example of Childe's rare interest in non-Western cultures and of what would remain his always highly qualified willingness to formulate cross-cultural generalizations.

Childe's studies of settlement patterns and burial practices reveal an interest in issues relating to prehistoric social and political behaviour resembling those that would characterize social and processual archaeology beginning in the 1960s. Yet, when he wrote *The prehistory of European society* (1958c) in the last months of his life, he was very pessimistic about the likelihood of archaeologists being able to discover ways to learn much about prehistoric social and political behaviour. Childe found his thinking trapped by the typological approach that had characterized his research since the 1920s. He did not recall his settlement research of the 1940s and clearly had not read Gordon Willey's (1953) major study of changing settlement patterns in the Viru Valley of Peru, which had been published four years earlier. Childe and most other British archaeologists were largely unaware of what was going on in American archaeology at this period, a situation vastly different from today. Childe's inability to discover ways to make progress in the social and political interpretation of archaeological data probably helped to convince him that his intellect was failing. This, combined with his concern about other medical problems and his general despondence about growing old, in turn seem to have played a major rôle in his decision to hurl himself to his death from Govett's Leap, in New South Wales, on 19 October 1957.

We can only speculate about the sort of mental block that was preventing Childe from realizing that he had already transcended typological analysis in his studies of prehistoric settlements and burial practices. It appears to be the same kind of block that led him, in *The prehistory of European society*, to attribute to Christopher Hawkes the idea that many distinctive and progressive features of European culture had already been apparent in the Bronze Age (Childe 1958c: 8). Such a view had been an important element in the first edition of *The dawn of European civilization*. It is possible that Childe's latter-day fears about his diminishing creativity were based on an accurate assessment of his mental state.

Evolutionary archaeology

We must next consider Childe's later, overtly theoretical writings. Childe had been a socialist since his undergraduate days at the University of Sydney, when he openly rebelled against his conservative family background. He was active in the anti-conscription movement during the First World War and later was private secretary to John Storey, who became the first Labor premier of New South Wales in 1920 (cf. Mulvaney, this volume). His first book, *How Labour governs* (1923), written after the fall of the Labor government, was an important case study of the co-optation of Labor politicians by the establishment in a parliamentary democracy (Gathercole 1989). Childe had planned to write a second book dealing with the history of the Australian Labor Party, but appears to have begun to pursue archaeology as a full-time career before he started it.

Childe's early culture–historical studies arranged modes of thought that were already current in archaeology in new and innovative patterns, but I fail to detect any significant political bias of his own in these works. Even his early economic studies drew upon conventional archaeological theorizing and exhibited only minimal signs of Marxist or social democratic influences. Childe's Marxist friends and his occasional political writings attest that he already had at least a basic understanding of Marxism at this period (Dutt 1957), so this omission cannot be ascribed to a lack of awareness. It seems as if at this time Childe was trying to distance himself from his political past and to forge a career for himself as an archaeologist. Given the conservative orientation of most British archaeologists at that period, he no doubt made a wise decision. It is unlikely that an outspoken Marxist would have been offered the Abercromby Chair at the University of Edinburgh or any other substantial university post in 1927.

Childe was drawn back into the political fray by two events, one political and one personal. The first was Hitler's coming to power in Germany in 1933. Childe was convinced that archaeologists outside Germany had to counteract the propagandistic uses that were being made of archaeology by the Nazi Party. The second event was his first visit to the Soviet Union in 1935, where he was impressed by the extent of government support for archaeological research and the use of its findings for public education. Childe later claimed that he was also impressed by the ways that Soviet archaeologists were using social and political factors to explain technological change. This led him in the direction of what was later to be called social archaeology (Renfrew 1973b), and more specifically to consider how the relations of production influenced cultural change. It also induced him to adopt a cultural-evolutionary perspective, which had been out of favour among Western European archaeologists since the 1880s.

The adoption of an explicitly Marxist perspective also may have enhanced

17

his views about the rôle played by women in the development of culture. While he initially characterized women as being especially reluctant to adopt innovations (Childe 1934: 105), he soon reversed his position and observed that they probably had invented many processes, including the manufacture of pottery and cloth, which were the most complex technologies known in early Neolithic times (Childe 1942a: 51–2). However, his specific examples were derived from the writings of other "bourgeois" archaeologists rather than inspired by the feminism of Friedrich Engels.

Yet Childe was very critical of Soviet archaeology and he rejected many aspects of it that did not accord with his understanding of the archaeological record and scientific method (cf. Klejn: this volume). He did not accept the unilinear evolutionary scheme, roughly based on Engels's *The origin of the family, private property and the state*, that was being propagated throughout the Soviet Union and had been imposed upon archaeology by the politically powerful linguist Nicholai Marr. Childe argued that the concept of unilinear evolution ran totally contrary to the highly distinct courses of social development that were documented in the archaeological records of the Near East, Egypt and Europe (Childe 1944: 23).

Childe also objected to the rejection of diffusion and migration as factors promoting cultural change. In *Scotland before the Scots* (1946a), he admitted that Western archaeologists had probably relied too heavily on these processes as explanations of change and paid too little attention to internal factors. He also maintained that Marxist concepts were very useful for explaining socio-political change in prehistoric Scotland. Yet he affirmed that archaeologists could never account for the Neolithic period without also accepting that, until domesticated plants and animals had been brought into Scotland from the southeast, a food-producing economy could not have developed there (Childe 1946a: 24).

Childe also expressed grave doubts about the adequacy of some Soviet interpretations of archaeological evidence, such as treating female figurines as evidence of a matriarchal clan society. More generally, he mistrusted the unilinear evolutionist assumption that societies at the same level of development, even if they were historically unrelated, would be fundamentally similar. He was shocked by Soviet archaeology's repudiation of typological analysis on the grounds that it was a manifestation of bourgeois formalism; rightly fearing that this would inhibit the construction of cultural chronologies (Daniel 1958: 66).

Finally, Childe refused to accept that the Soviet government had the right to tell archaeologists how they should interpret archaeological data; instead he maintained that Soviet archaeologists should be encouraged to test Marxist ideas against archaeological data in order to see whether these ideas could be sustained or required modification (Childe 1951: 28–9). While Childe, unlike most other Western archaeologists, was prepared to learn from Soviet archaeologists, his sense of professional integrity and his archaeological knowledge took precedence over his political sympathies. Because of this, while Soviet archaeology significantly influenced Childe's work, it never did so in a dogmatic fashion.

Childe did not enjoy "giving comfort" to right-wing archaeologists by publicly airing his differences with Soviet colleagues; hence he often expressed his disapproval in an elliptical manner and more often by example than by words. This has led hostile analysts to assume that he was a more dogmatic Marxist than was actually the case. Childe was a significant Marxist scholar in the 1940s and 1950s, precisely because he refused to follow the party line and insisted on treating Marxism as "as way of thought, not a set of dogmas" (Morris 1957). This is evident in books that he wrote during the 1940s and 1950s.

In *What happened in history*, Childe (1942a) examined the rôle of technology in bringing about social change, but he also insisted that technological change had to be understood as occurring within specific social, economic, and political contexts. More specifically, he argued that in some societies at every level of development conservative religious beliefs and political systems have played an important rôle in impeding social change. Hence he viewed the superstructures of societies as being historically significant, but only in the negative sense that they can impede social progress. In particular, he saw superstructures being utilized by dominant groups and social classes as a means to protect their collective privileges. Yet he believed that, while in some societies high-status groups might succeed in doing this for long periods, such goals could be achieved only at the expense of weakening these societies vis-à-vis more flexible neighbouring groups.

In *Social evolution*, Childe (1951) examined how environmental differences and dissimilar antecedent Mesolithic cultural traditions had produced highly distinctive early Neolithic societies in various regions of Europe and the Near East, even though all of these societies had adopted the same complex of domesticated plants and animals and the same set of behavioural patterns that was associated with caring for them. He argued that, even if in the long run every economic base had the power to shape a superstructure that accorded perfectly with its needs, long before such an equilibrium could be reached, the relationship between base and superstructure would have been disrupted by still more technological innovations, which tended to diffuse rapidly from one society to another. Hence every prehistoric culture was influenced in random and unpredictable ways by its historical antecedents and by the vagaries of diffusion, no less than it was shaped by its relations of production. Childe pointed out that no-one could account for the nature of parliamentary government in 19th-century Britain solely in terms of the prevailing capitalist mode of production (Childe 1936: 98). While he refrained from publicly attacking the work of Leslie White and Julian Steward, whom he recognized as fellow exponents of materialistic and evolutionary views of cultural systems (Childe 1946b), his Marxist approach was more subtle and nuanced, and took account of more factors influencing cultural change than did either White's technological determinism or Steward's ecologism.

While *What happened in history* was Childe's most widely read book and probably remains the most widely read book ever written by an archaeologist, his evolutionary studies had little impact on the discipline of archaeology, and most professional archaeologists seem to have misunderstood their general thrust. In Britain, his evolutionary publications were generally dismissed as theoretically inconsequential popularizing by an expert on European prehistory. In the United States, Childe was recognized as an evolutionist, but his Marxist ideas aroused fear and resentment in an academic community that was both threatened and influenced by McCarthyism (cf. Flannery, this volume). It is apparent that few American anthropologists bothered to read Childe's works closely. Otherwise Steward (1953) would not have found it so easy to persuade a generation of American anthropologists that Childe was nothing more than a latter-day exponent of the ideas of 19th-century unilinear evolutionism. Childe's research on problems of social evolution did, however, raise questions that required more knowledge about prehistoric social and political institutions and religious beliefs. This in turn encouraged the development of social and processual archaeology (cf. Renfrew, this volume). It also helped to renew the relationship between archaeology and anthropology, which in Europe had been disrupted following the decline of interest in cultural evolutionism in the late 19th century.

Symbolic archaeology

The second distinctive wave of Childe's theoretical studies began in the early 1940s and continued through the final decade of his life. While he was alive, this was the least understood, or even known, phase of his researches. Judged by the reviews of his publications, Childe appears to have been addressing posterity rather than contemporary archaeologists. In the 1940s, he was angered by the Soviet Union entering into the Hitler–Stalin pact, although he admitted this to only a few like-minded friends. He was also disillusioned by the declining quality of Soviet archaeology, which as a consequence of its rejection of the typological method had failed to produce a convincing cultural chronology for the prehistoric period. As a result, Childe ceased to look to Soviet archaeology for inspiration and began to read Marxist and related philosophical writings in order to acquire a better understanding of Marxism as a philosophical system. The principal result of this research was that Childe gained a deeper appreciation of the rôle that knowledge and beliefs played in cultural change. This encouraged him to attempt to transcend the limitations of both materialist and idealist approaches, as they were formulated in the 1940s, by demonstrating that beliefs can best be accounted for in relation to a more holistic materialistic perspective.

Childe agreed that all human behaviour is guided by knowledge, some of which is acquired through direct experience but most of which is transmitted to individuals as members of societies. He also posited that human beings do not adapt to the environment as it actually is but rather to the environment as they perceive it to be. Each individual carries about in her or his mind a "cultural map", incorporating knowledge acquired through learning and experience, from which that individual selects the data required to adapt to the social and natural environment. As conditions change and old behavioural patterns are perceived to be maladaptive, they are modified as a result of innumerable individual decisions and changes in public policy. Most behavioural patterns that remain adaptive persist unchallenged for generations (Childe 1949, 1956a, 1979).

Yet, while action is based on what is believed to be true rather than on material reality, Childe argued that normally there is enough congruence between the two to ensure the physical survival and reproduction of human groups. Moreover, while the body depends upon the mind for its survival, without a living body the mind cannot exist. This creates strong selective pressures which ensure that in the normal course of events there will be enough congruence between beliefs about reality, and reality itself, to ensure the survival of human groups. On the other hand, because each society confronts new problems with its existing store of knowledge and behavioural patterns and in most instances these alter only sufficiently to cope with new external problems and to repress or resolve internal contradictions, historical traditions play a major rôle in shaping human history. Since these traditions and the problems that challenge their efficacy tend to arise adventitiously, the course of human history is highly contingent. Thus, while what has happened in the past can be explained, what is likely to happen in the future can be predicted only with considerable uncertainty, even in the short run (Childe 1947, 1979). In this way, Childe applied to archaeology Marx's dictum that "human beings make their own history . . . not under conditions chosen by themselves, but ones directly encountered, given, and transmitted from the past" (Marx 1852 in Marx & Engels 1962, vol. 1: 247).

By identifying cultural evolution as what really happens, rather than with an idealized trajectory or even some elaborate multi-linear scheme, Childe was expressing his belief that cultural development occurs in a multi-linear fashion and that the nature of the factors that promote and inhibit cultural change in specific societies is largely unpredictable. In spite of this, he never abandoned his belief that, if technological progress continues, societies will evolve in some general manner from primitive egalitarianism through class exploitation to a socialist paradise. Unlike many of the more doctrinaire Marxists in the Soviet Union, he did not maintain that every society necessarily participates in this progress, that major setbacks do not occur, that progress cannot be blocked for indefinite periods by reactionary forces, or that a catastrophe, such as nuclear war, might not destroy humanity (Childe 1947).

As a Marxist, Childe also distinguished between true consciousness, which permits the effective manipulation of the external world, and false consciousness, which only gives the illusion of doing so. Childe maintained that technology provided the clearest example of true consciousness, even if preindustrial technologies often incorporated rituals that in fact contributed nothing positive to the mechanical processes involved. By contrast, religious beliefs and magic provided the clearest examples of false consciousness. The main rôle of false consciousness was to supply human beings with a feeling of security in situations where technological control was inadequate and to facilitate social interaction by trying to represent acts of exploitation as natural or inevitable in the minds of both the exploiters and their victims. True and false consciousness can be distinguished only in retrospect, since the efficacy of false consciousness depends upon it not being recognized as such.

Childe maintained that true consciousness constitutes practical knowledge, which accumulates over time and by means of diffusion becomes the heritage of all human beings, while false consciousness perishes with the individual society or cultural tradition that produced it (Childe 1956a). As a rationalist, Childe remained convinced that all human beings would eventually discover that burning garbage was a more effective way to prevent disease than burning witches (Childe 1956a: 59–60, 106). He also maintained that, because of its rationality and efficacy, true consciousness could be reconstructed for all prehistoric societies, using the universal generalizations of modern physics, chemistry and biology to explain archaeological evidence pertaining to ancient technologies. On the other hand, false consciousness could be understood only by means of cultural traditions that were historically related to the societies being studied.

Archaeologists could utilize knowledge derived from the physical sciences to reconstruct the scientific techniques by means of which bronze-casting had been carried out in a particular prehistoric society. Yet, if archaeological evidence revealed that the process had involved the slaughter of a goat, they could not determine precisely what the prehistoric smiths had intended that this action should accomplish. That would be possible only if written records were available that explained this custom or if knowledge of sacrifices had survived in related cultures that could provide insights into what this act might have meant (Childe 1956b: 45).

Childe drew from these arguments a further conclusion that today disturbs many post-processual archaeologists, but which was perfectly in accord with his Marxist evolutionary beliefs. He argued that, by providing first and foremost a history of technological progress, archaeology sheds light on the most important aspects of human development, while, by failing to preserve a detailed record of prehistoric religious beliefs, the archaeological record merely casts into oblivion the memories of human ignorance and folly (Childe 1956b: 172). In his rhetoric, Childe failed to take account of the fact that the evidence of religious behaviour, in the form of temples and tombs, looms very large in the archaeological record and reveals much about the concerns of prehistoric peoples even in the absence of any detailed knowledge of their specific beliefs (Trigger 1990). He also forgot his earlier claim that religion had played a major, if purely negative, rôle throughout human history (Childe 1936, 1942a). His conclusions did suggest, however, that Hawkes's (1954) ladder of difficulty, which maintained that, from purely archaeological data, it was harder to infer religious behaviour than economic activities , did not imply as important a loss as Hawkes and other idealists had feared. These conclusions accorded with the materialistic, evolutionary beliefs that were increasingly in the ascendant in the 1950s.

As a Marxist, Childe was keenly aware of the subjective nature of knowledge, which in part explains why he greatly admired the work of R. G. Collingwood (1939, 1946). He also believed that knowledge was a social construction that changed as the conditions of human life changed. Yet he would have had little sympathy for those modern archaeologists who, sometimes in the name of Marxism, seek to reduce all human knowledge to the level of self-serving fantasies and who deny that there is any way that theories about human behaviour can ever be objectively tested (Shanks & Tilley 1987a,b). He believed that, over time, progressive human societies achieve a more accurate mental approximation of the real world, which permits human beings to relate to that world more effectively (Childe 1956a: 54). While acknowledging that far greater difficulties are involved in achieving an objective, if partial, understanding of human behaviour, Childe did not doubt that over time archaeologists could learn more about the material basis of life in the past and about how cultures had changed over long periods. That in turn, he believed, would allow archaeologists to contribute to a "science of progress" that would help human beings to control their social environment better, even if it could not become an exact or mathematical science (Childe 1947: 1–3). For Childe, as a Marxist theorist, the true value of archaeology lay not in the many different propagandistic uses that were being made of its findings (most of which he regarded as evil), but in its capacity to achieve an increasingly objective understanding of the past that might result in a better future for all humanity.

During Childe's lifetime, little attention was paid to his writings about the nature of culture. He himself did not suggest any practical applications of these ideas to archaeological analysis, as he had done in the case of societal analysis with his pioneering of settlement studies and his adaptations of Soviet ideas concerning the social interpretation burial data. He did not assign the symbolic aspects of material culture an active rôle in bringing about social change, but stressed their rôle in resisting change. Finally he remained a committed materialist. Hence many of his ideas about the rôle of culture do not accord with what modern idealists (including many neo-Marxists) believe about material culture (Hodder 1982). His faith in science also appears out of step with the siren call of intellectual anarchism that is currently attracting some archaeologists. In spite of this, Childe's discussions of culture in the last decade of his life clearly adumbrated the cognitive and symbolic concerns of the post-processual archaeology that emerged in the 1980s.

Conclusion

I have tried to provide some indication of the range and creativity, as well as the limitations, of Childe's thought. He contributed to the three main archaeological movements of the 20th century: culture–historical, processual, and post-processual. He was one of the founders and chief exponents of culture–historical archaeology, but he quickly became aware of the dangers of cultural determinism – a lesson that post-processual archaeologists are in danger of having to relearn. Both before and after he began to base his work on Marxist concepts, he helped to pioneer the political and economic approaches that in the 1960s came to play a major rôle in processual archaeology. He did not, however, develop a strong interest in cultural ecology, which throughout his life he continued to view from a possibilist perspective. Finally, in the last years of his life, he developed an interest in cultural behaviour that anticipated many of the current concerns of post-processual archaeology.

The dynamic qualities of Childe's thought indicate why his work has remained of more than historical interest. At the beginning and the end of his career, Childe, as a culture–historical and a prototypical post-processual archaeologist, stressed in very different ways the importance of the knowledge possessed by human beings as a significant factor in bringing about cultural change. In the course of his research, he realized that it was necessary to take account of ecological, social, and political relations as elements that played an important rôle in transforming cultural systems. He was able to posit the dialectical relationship between these factors in such a way that he avoided the twin impasses of ecological and cultural determinism. His rationalist and materialist perspective on human behaviour remains a viable, though not in the present idealist era a favoured, approach. While he may not have provided answers that modern archaeologists find satisfactory, he challenged colleagues of his own and succeeding decades by constructing a vision of archaeology that was as broad as that of the other social sciences, but which also took account of the particular strengths and limitations of archaeological data.

Archaeologists who came after Childe have continued to make vital contributions to the interpretation of archaeological data and have expanded the archaeological database in every part of the world. Yet the continuing struggle between processual and post-processual archaeology reveals that in doing so they often adopted a vision of human behaviour that was narrower, more deterministic, and I believe further removed from reality than was Childe's. Today, an increasing number of archaeologists are reaching the conclusion that the way forwards lies not in partisan adherence to the tenets of culture–historical, processual, or post-processual archaeology but in some kind of critical synthesis of all three modes of explanation (Preucel 1991). If that is so, the spirit, if not the letter, of Childe's approach can still help to guide the construction of a more satisfactory theoretical framework for the interpretation of archaeological data.

Acknowledgements

The research on which this paper was based was carried out while the author held a Killam Research Fellowship administered by the Canada Council. The paper was finished while he enjoyed sabbatical leave from McGill University. Travel to the conference was financed by a McGill Travel Grant for International Conferences, made possible by funds from the Social Sciences and Humanities Research Council of Canada.

References

Binford, L. R. 1962. Archaeology as anthropology. *American Antiquity* **13**, 170–89.
Binford, L. R. & J. A. Sabloff. 1982. Paradigms, systematics, and archaeology. *Journal of Anthropological Research* **38**, 137–53.
Bradley, R. 1984. *The social foundations of prehistoric Britain*. London: Longman.
Chapman, R. 1990. *Emerging complexity: the later prehistory of south-east Spain, Iberia, and the west Mediterranean*. Cambridge: Cambridge University Press.
Childe, V. G. 1923. *How Labour governs*. London: Labour Publishing Company.
    1925. *The dawn of European civilization*. London: Kegan Paul, Trench, Trubner.
    1926. *The Aryans: a study of Indo-European origins*. London: Kegan Paul, Trench, Trubner.
    1928. *The most ancient East: the oriental prelude to European prehistory*. London: Kegan Paul, Trench, Trubner.
    1929. *The Danube in prehistory*. Oxford: Oxford University Press.
    1930. *The Bronze Age*. Cambridge: Cambridge University Press.
    1931. *Skara Brae: a Pictish village in Orkney*. London: Kegan Paul, Trench, Trubner.
    1933a. Is prehistory practical? *Antiquity* **7**, 410–18.
    1933b. Races, peoples and cultures in prehistoric Europe. *History* **18**, 193–203.
    1934. *New light on the most ancient East*. London: Kegan Paul, Trench, Trubner.
    1935. *The prehistory of Scotland*. London: Kegan Paul, Trench, Trubner.
    1936. *Man makes himself*. London: Watts.
    1940. *Prehistoric communities of the British Isles*. London: Chambers.
    1942a. *What happened in history*. Harmondsworth: Penguin (page numbers cited from first American edition, 1946).
    1942b. The chambered cairns of Rousay. *Antiquaries Journal* **22**, 139–42.
    1944. Archaeological ages as technological stages. *Royal Anthropological Institute, Journal* **74**, 7–24.
    1945. Directional changes in funerary practices during 50,000 years. *Man* **45**, 13–19.
    1946a. *Scotland before the Scots*. London: Methuen.
    1946b. Archaeology and anthropology. *Southwestern Journal of Anthropology* **2**, 243–51.
    1947. *History*. London: Cobbett Press.
    1949. *Social worlds of knowledge*. London: Oxford University Press.
    1950. The urban revolution. *The Town Planning Review* **21**, 3–17.

1951. *Social evolution*. New York: Schuman.

1956a. *Society and knowledge*. New York: Harper.

1956b. *Piecing together the past*. London: Routledge & Kegan Paul.

1958a. Retrospect. *Antiquity* 32, 69–74.

1958b. Valediction. *Bulletin of the Institute of Archaeology, University of London* 1, 1–8.

1958c. *The prehistory of European society*. Harmondsworth: Penguin.

1979. Prehistory and Marxism. *Antiquity* 53, 93–5.

Clark, J. G. D. 1939. *Archaeology and society*. London: Methuen.

1952. *Prehistoric Europe: the economic basis*. London: Methuen.

1954. *Excavations at Star Carr*. Cambridge: Cambridge University Press.

1961. *World prehistory: an outline*. Cambridge: Cambridge University Press.

1976. Prehistory since Childe. *Bulletin of the Institute of Archaeology, University of London* 13, 1–21.

Collingwood, R. G. 1939. *An autobiography*. Oxford: Oxford University Press.

1946. *The idea of history*. Oxford: Oxford University Press.

Daniel, G. 1958 Editorial. *Antiquity* 32, 65–68.

Dutt, R. P. 1957. Tribute to memory of Gordon Childe. *Daily Worker*, 22 October: 3.

Gathercole, P. 1984. A consideration of ideology. In *Marxist perspectives in archaeology*, M. Spriggs (ed.), 149–54. Cambridge: Cambridge University Press.

1989. Childe's early Marxism. In *Critical traditions in contemporary archaeology*, V. Pinsky & A. Wylie (eds), 80–7. Cambridge: Cambridge University Press.

Green, S. 1981. *Prehistorian: a biography of V. Gordon Childe*. Bradford-on-Avon, England: Moonraker Press.

Hawkes, C. F. C. 1954. Archeological theory and method: some suggestions from the Old World. *American Anthropologist* 56, 155–68.

Hodder, I. 1982. *Symbols in action*. Cambridge: Cambridge University Press.

1990. *The domestication of Europe: structure and contingency in Neolithic societies*. Oxford: Basil Blackwell.

Kohl, P. L. 1984. Force, history and the evolutionist paradigm. In *Marxist perspectives in archaeology*, M. Spriggs (ed.), 127–34. Cambridge: Cambridge University Press.

Kruglov, A. P. & G. V. Podgayetskij, 1935. *Rodovoe obshchestvo stepei vostochnoi Evropy*. Leningrad: Izvestiia GAIMK, no. 119.

Kus, S. M. 1983. The social representation of space: dimensioning the cosmological and the quotidian. In *Archaeological hammers and theories*, J. A. Moore & A. S. Keene (eds), 277–98. New York: Academic Press.

1984. The spirit and its burden: archaeology and symbolic activity. In *Marxist perspectives in archaeology*, M. Spriggs (ed), 101–7. Cambridge: Cambridge University Press.

Leone, M. P. (ed.) 1972. *Contemporary archaeology*. Carbondale, Illinois: Southern Illinois University Press.

Marx, K. & F. Engels 1962. *Selected works in two volumes*. Moscow: Foreign Languages Publishing House.

Morris, J. 1957. Gordon Childe. *Past and Present* 12, 2.

Preucel, R. W. (ed.) 1991. *Processual and postprocessual archaeologies: multiple ways of knowing the past*. Carbondale, Illinois: Center for Archaeological Investigation, Occasional Paper no. 10.

Renfrew, A. C. 1972. *The emergence of civilisation: the Cyclades and the Aegean in the third millennium B.C.* London: Methuen.

1973a. *Before civilization: the radiocarbon revolution and prehistoric Europe*. London: Cape.

1973b. *Social archaeology*. Southampton: The University.

Renfrew, A. C. & S. Shennan (eds) 1982. *Ranking, resource and exchange: aspects of the archaeology of early European society*. Cambridge: Cambridge University Press.

Rouse, I. 1972. *Introduction to prehistory*. New York: McGraw-Hill.

Rowlands, M., M. Larsen & K. Kristiansen (eds) 1987. *Center and periphery in the ancient world*. Cambridge: Cambridge University Press.

Shanks, M. & C. Tilley 1987a. *Re-constructing archaeology: theory and practice*. Cambridge: Cambridge University Press.

1987b. *Social theory and archaeology*. Cambridge: Polity Press.

Sherratt, A. 1989. V. Gordon Childe: archaeology and intellectual history. *Past and Present* **125**, 151–85.

Spriggs, M. 1977. Where the hell are we? (or a young man's quest). In *Archaeology and anthropology*, M. Spriggs (ed.), 3–17. Oxford: BAR Supplementary Series, 19.

Steward, J. H. 1953. Evolution and process. In *Anthropology today*, A. L. Kroeber (ed.), 313–26. Chicago: University of Chicago Press.

1955. *Theory of culture change*. Urbana: University of Illinois Press.

Trigger, B. G. 1990. Monumental architecture: a thermodynamic explanation of symbolic behaviour. *World Archaeology* **22**, 119–32.

Wells, P. S. 1984. *Farms, villages, and cities: commerce and urban origins in late prehistoric Europe*. Ithaca, New York: Cornell University Press.

Whittle, A. W. R. 1985. *Neolithic Europe: a survey*. Cambridge: Cambridge University Press.

Willey, G. R. 1953. *Prehistoric settlement patterns in the Virú Valley, Peru*. Washington: Bureau of American Ethnology, Bulletin 135.

Discussion

CHAIRED BY DAVID HARRIS

Hood: Both in your book and just now you said that Gordon Childe was influenced by Sir Arthur Evans during the time that he was at Oxford. I only remember him mentioning Evans once, and then in a favourable way over the date of the final destruction of Knossos. He said that he would trust Evans far more than he would [Duncan] Mackenzie. I wondered if there was positive evidence that he did, in fact, know Evans and Mackenzie and also if one can say in what way Evans influenced his thinking at that time?

Trigger: The biographical details I don't know, because, as you realize my basic concern is to analyze his writings. It is clear however that the fundamental formulation of *The dawn*, which has the idea of material culture coming from the Near East being transformed within the European context by the genius of the Indo-Europeans, is derived from J. L. Myres. Indeed, the title of Childe's book echoes the title of Myres's *The dawn of history*, published in 1911. He does occasionally cite some of Evans's general papers, in which Evans expounds the same view. Although Myres's and Evans's views on this differ in detail, they were very similar in terms of the general idea that they were expressing, and that was certainly something that Childe absorbed in the atmosphere of Oxford.

Renfrew: May I add a specific point to that? I think it is clear that Childe was very much influenced by the success of Evans in periodizing the site at Knossos. In fact I think that the periodization which Childe developed in *The Danube in prehistory* was quite explicitly and consciously based on Evans's success in taking Vinča as the essential starting-point; and there was a paper in *Antiquity* in 1927 in which Childe acknowledges that he is using Vinča for a basic periodization of Europe and very much taking a leaf out of the Evans book in doing so.

Green: Just to say that I believe that one of Childe's supervisors for his B Litt at Oxford was Sir Arthur Evans.

Gathercole: I would like to make a general point and then give a couple of quotations from Childe on his philosophical standpoint, but I would like first of all to thank Bruce Trigger for an admirable lecture and say that, to me personally, it is magnificent that both he and Sally Green are here – I don't know if Barbara McNairn is also – but their publications at the beginning of the 1980s were the foundation for all subsequent work on Childe and all three of them are extremely important.

On the question of the dichotomy between Childe's stance in 1925 and his stance later on, particularly as exemplified in the changes of emphasis in the successive editions of *The dawn*, I came to the view a couple of years ago that the first edition is actually Hegelian. The paradox is that, philosophically, Childe was I believe a Marxist from very early days. He contacted all sorts of people in Oxford, such as G. D. H. Cole and Palme Dutt, which exemplifies the point, as does his subsequent political experience in Australia. Archaeologically, I think that he adopted a sort of Hegelian attitude by filling in, in idealistic terms, interpretations that he could not provide from archaeological data – these came later, in the subsequent editions of the book. And one of the paradoxes here is that, like Hegel and like Marx, he was a great historian of capitalism, of the genesis of capitalism. I think that this is all part of the way he saw his rôle in studying the subject over the full span of his career, and I think we can see more than the genesis of that in the 1920s.

I would just like to tuck in two quotations of his *vis-à-vis* the permutations of his political attitudes, which I think were much more influenced by current politics than many archaeologists have recognized. Here is what he says in a letter to Palme Dutt in October 1938, just after the Münich crisis:

> To me Marxism means effectively a way of approach to and a methodological device for the interpretation of archaeological and historical material and I accept it because and in so far as it *works*. (and "works" is underlined)

In other words, it is gradualism that he is suggesting here in the use of the material, and he makes the point specifically later in the paragraph vis à vis *Man makes himself*. He says (I paraphrase somewhat),

"If I *began* as a Marxist" – that is, as an explicit Marxist – "my colleagues and students would not listen to me, but they are led round, as it were, by the argument within *Man makes himself*, not by the pejorative statements that might, as it were, preface it."

And, let me make one point in relation to the whole question of the sociology of knowledge. In 1950, Meyer Fortes spoke on the concept of culture in a discussion at the British Association which was published in *Nature*. Childe was there among the social psychologists and anthropologists, etc., and Fortes, who knew him well and liked him very much, summarized Childe's contribution like this:

> Artefacts are the fossilized remains of cultures such as can still be observed by anthropologists, and symbolize patterns of behaviour learnt within social groups just as language and custom is learnt. Though much is missing, an attempt can be made to reconstruct these behaviour patterns. But we have still to face the full difficulties of the concept. Culture conditions values and categories. The good, the true and the beautiful are relative categories given by society. We are bound to the frame of reference derived from our own culture and we are unable to get outside of it.

Trigger: Fortes's paper is very interesting because, when I reviewed the history of archaeological thought [1989], it was clear that one of the things that had gone on in archaeology as a whole was that, while new ideas develop and spread, they don't necessarily immediately replace old ones. We are not dealing here with a kind of intellectual layer-cake. Certain ideas begin to balloon and expand, and others may shrink, but the others remain active in very curious ways. As I was writing this paper it occurred to me that this was also the case in Childe's life, that certain ideas at different points began to get hold of him and to reorganize the way he was thinking about things. But old ideas would, in fragmentary ways, survive and become an important part of the next stage of what he was doing.

You raised another point, which is that the political events that were going on around Childe, and also the people that he happened to be meeting or reading at any particular time, come into his work. Sometimes it is a flash in the pan – their influence will be expressed in one or two papers and then disappear; at other times, their influence persists and becomes important. What one has ultimately is a very complicated but total corpus of Childe's thought made up of many bits and pieces. I would be the first to admit that my paper has only attempted to capture reality at what you might call a middle level of what was going on. But there are many different levels.

Referring to the point that you made about the Hegelian-ness of his first period – I must say that, approaching as I did from an internalist point of view, it seems to me that in that early period, which includes not only *The dawn* and *The Danube* but also everything down to *The Bronze Age*, you can in fact show that his work contains almost nothing but combinations and permutations of existing ideas from within the canon of archaeological thought at that period. It is on that basis that I said that it impressed me as being highly non-ideological, in the sense that it was stimulated from outside the existing corpus of Marxist ideology. That you can see an Hegelian influence here is interesting, but that also needs to be discussed. It certainly seems to me that in that period Childe was working as a craftsman within the discipline. It is after 1933 and 1935 that you start to get a greater openness to what is going on in society and what is going on in other disciplines. At that point, it becomes necessary to analyze, on an article-by-article basis, what the influences on Childe were and how they affected his thought. It is not a study I would like to do myself, but certainly a biographer or someone interested in the history and philosophy of science would find it a fascinating subject.

Harris: You emphasize the complexity of the Childe corpus, I am sure rightly. But one of the points that strikes me is that he apparently showed so little awareness of what was going on in [biological] ecology, as opposed to cultural ecology, at the time. You mention his awareness, one might say, his dismissal of Julian Steward. Is it not surprising that – working in Britain, which after all contributed some of the founding concepts to ecology, through Tansley and others – he was not influenced by this body of knowledge and its concepts? Is that right, and, if so, can you account for it?

Trigger: I think it is right and in fact I had an extra paragraph in here, which I cut out because I did not want to bore people! It seems to me that there are two points: one of the things that seems not to have changed during the course of his life was that he was a possibilist. Occasionally, he would say nice things about ecology to people whom he knew and respected, and who had done something that he admired, but fundamentally his attitude was that it was limiting although not determining. And I think that, as his thinking became more Marxist, the idea that the determining factors were social, rather than non-social or environmental, helped to keep him on a possibilist path through the whole of his life.

Now, that does not mean that he did not come up with some surprising conclusions in other areas. For example, it is seldom remarked on that his last book, *The prehistory of European society*, is in fact a paeon of praise to free enterprise. In that book it is after all the smiths, who were wandering about, not shackled to any workshop as they were in Oriental despotisms, who created progress and civilization. This was a very surprising conclusion for someone to come up with who is at the same time praising Stalin and the early postwar Soviet state. So, there are areas in which Childe was clearly not shackled by the prevailing Marxist tradition. He could exclude ideas by not writing about subjects he was not inclined to think important. This evidently applied to ecology. You have touched on one of the things he didn't think about and which is a weakness in his work, just as it became a strength in the work of Grahame Clark and other people, who made ecology a very central part of British archaeology.

30

Saunders: It is very interesting, this point about Childe's Marxism. Your work in general suggests not only the influence of Soviet Marxism on Childe but also his critical attitude to it, not only on the political level but also with the theory of determinism, and its assumption of inevitable changes. His attitude is remarkable, given the intellectual context of the 1930s, when Marxism was Soviet Marxism, dominated by Stalin, and the different Marxisms that we have today did not exist.

However, the question that I would like to pose is to what extent did Childe actually break theoretically from Soviet Marxism and its underpinning in a very mechanical materialism, because, although he was critical of it, the notion of technological change and inevitable revolutions seems ultimately to underpin his work. In *What happened in history*, for example, the only really Marxist reference is to Stalin. So, in one sense, Childe was critical and understood the subjectivity of knowledge, which was being discussed by Soviet archaeologists, but he nevertheless failed to develop an alternative to Soviet Marxism. What is your reaction to that?

Trigger: Childe's friends, who describe him attending union meetings, say that he sat there but never said anything, and people who describe him going to Marxist political activities also say that he sat and listened but never spoke. He was very dependent on the few, carefully mediated social relations he had with people. Many of these relations were mediated through his participation in Communist Party activities, and – just as he was anxious to appear the sort of person who anybody he had a personal relationship with wanted him to be – he was very anxious not to upset these people. It is, therefore, very interesting that, although he quickly developed a critique of what he thought was right and wrong in Soviet archaeology – and you can find it expressed obliquely if you look for it – it was not something that he came out with and was prepared to discuss openly. My own guess, although it is only a guess, is that the explanation for this is that he did not want to lose these ties that he had with people which made his life a little more pleasant and more human. So one of the prices that he paid was not saying very much on a lot of issues about which he might have had a great deal to say that was interesting.

On the issue of his relationship with the Marxism of the Second Internationale, as it was expounded in the Soviet Union, there are two points: one is that I think there are many points that modern neo-Marxists would like him to have disagreed with, such as the distinction between true and false consciousness, which clearly he thought was useful. Secondly, he did in fact exhibit in his writings a fascination with the question of why change did not occur, namely how false consciousness works to keep systems working that were based upon injustice, inequity and inefficiency. Why did they survive for very, very long periods?

At that time Childe was asking questions that his Marxist colleagues were not asking. In the Soviet Union the suppression of the concept of the Asiatic mode of production, which was done as a political favour to the Communist Party in China at that period, had precluded discussion of a whole set of issues about why change did not occur in certain kinds of societies. Childe, either out of innocence or because he felt that these were important issues, just went ahead and discussed them. Indeed, he made them a central part of *What happened in history* and the whole set of writings that follow on from it. So he, in fact, discussed issues which were not discussed in Soviet Russia at the time and were even forbidden to be discussed, such as the Asiatic mode of production, the very mention of which disappeared from Soviet works on Marxism. So, I think it is unfair to say that he did not develop his own view: his view was different and it bothered people. George Thomson protested "Why is he not finding evidence of class struggle?" in these early societies. I think the answer is quite clear. He said that the ways in which these societies operated precluded the possibility of much class struggle by effectively dampening it down through a variety of social and political mechanisms. He was talking about these questions, he was saying things that were important, and yet he was saying them in a way that was polite enough for the Marxists of his day to say "he doesn't really understand these questions", rather than "he is actually discussing things that we are not allowed to discuss". Because his criticism of Soviet archaeology was extremely muted and polite, he did not create the confrontation with the orthodox Marxists that one might have expected. They could think that he did not quite know what he was talking about, that he did not understand things well enough; they did not have to accept that he was in fact offering a very deep criticism of current Marxist concepts about how societies and class consciousness operated.

The fact that Childe was making contributions in such a way that it did not look as though he was doing so has distracted attention from the importance of much of what he did. It also prevented some very interesting intellectual discussions taking place which might have driven him in ways that would have made his work much more creative and interesting at that period. This he was not prepared to do. I think it is because he really was emotionally dependent upon his associations with members of the British Communist Party – with the intellectuals who were members of the Party – and that the friendships that he had outside of his own discipline were simply too important for him. As human beings, we should understand somebody feeling that way. So here is another point to add to Peter Gathercole's: it is not only what Childe happened to read at a particular period, it is not only what was going on in the newspapers, it is also what kind of relationships he was having, not simply with archaeological colleagues but in the wider social world. Childe did not live an ordinary social life and having no wife and children he lacked the support of a family.

Bender: I have two comments, both of which refer to the end of each of the two sections in your paper (the first of which, I think you have really answered very adequately). I was unhappy with your suggestion that some-how intellectually Childe was failing and that was why the questions he had thought about early on in his career he could not bring back into conscious-ness and that therefore he could not really work. I think your answer to Tom Saunders actually gives much more of the complexity of what was hap-pening to Childe at that period. There may have been intellectual failing, but there was also a sort of impasse. This may have been partly because of these personal reasons or due to what was going on politically, but between a very profound understanding of the sociology of knowledge – which of course for more stringent Marxists would bring the superstructure down into discussion of infrastructure – and his desire to maintain a distinction between superstructure and infrastructure, between false consciousness and true consciousness, it seems to me there was an impasse. If he had lived a little longer and witnessed the intellectual developments of the late 1960s, when things opened up and discussions were freer and permissible, he might have been able to reconcile those concepts – he was in the wrong place at the right time at that moment in his life.

The second point relates to the end of your paper, where you suggested we should all get together: post-structuralists, processualists, post-processual-ists and culture historians. In a way, you have again answered that in your response to the question "Why didn't he talk ecology? Because he was a pos-sibilist". But there are some great ontological divisions which run right through these different positions and which I think make it very difficult to say, "Well, let's just stir the pot and we will come up with something that has a little bit of everything and that will be the best of all worlds".

Trigger: My only point would be that I suppose we all like to imagine that, had Childe lived into the present period of critical debate, he would have come up with what each of us personally believes. Reality is much more problematical and Childe produced real surprises. As I say, a man who ends up defending free enterprise within a Marxist theoretical framework must surprise people. But I see very little evidence of his having wanted to break down the distinction between infrastructure and superstructure, which was very important to him. He believed in superstructures but he regarded their rôles as essentially negative. And I think it would have taken a lot to shatter that belief. It was very deep rooted and of course it fitted the description of the world he knew most about.

References

Childe, V. G. 1927. The Danube thoroughfare and the beginnings of civilization in Europe. *Antiquity* 1, 79–91.

Fortes, M. 1950. The concept of culture. *Nature* 166, 711–13.

Myres, J. L. 1911. *The dawn of history*. London: Williams & Norgate.

Trigger, B. G. 1989. *A history of archaeological thought*. Cambridge: Cambridge University Press.

Childe and the archaeology of freedom

MICHAEL ROWLANDS

Perhaps I should first reassure you. I am not proposing yet another critique of evolutionary models in archaeology out of some misplaced reverence for the memory of Gordon Childe. Using the occasion to stand Childe on his head is not my intention, for the simple reason that I have no doubt that he was asking all the right questions and that these have contributed and still do contribute fundamentally to making archaeology the dynamic subject it is today.

In this spirit, I want to emphasize the ethical and moral imperatives of Childe's work since, it seems to me, we tend to gloss over, in a slightly embarrassed, rather English, manner the passions that drove the man in certain intellectual directions and gave his work profundity. By accepting the separation of his political stance from his academic writings we completely miss the fundamental commitment he had to the study of the past to explain the present so as to form an ethical choice for future action. In a straightforward and quite robust manner, Childe thought archaeology could inform us of how the past constrains and empowers our choice of action in the future. Compared to some general trends in anthropology at present, where authorship can be denied or displaced and where commitment to self-improvement seems to be a principal motive, there is every reason, it seems to me, for archaeologists to hold on to such clear-sighted goals.

Motivated by such moral imperatives, Childe can scarcely be accused of hiding political motives in his archaeological writings, even though the effects were cushioned by a rather scholarly academic separation of the popular political from the descriptive/archaeological. What motivated his archaeology was a vision of a particular kind of society and its future. Childe was very fond of quoting Marx in calling contemporary society "the closing chapter of the prehistoric stage of human society". In his little book *History* written in 1947 (Childe 1947a), he reiterated his belief in history as a creative process. Hegel is cited approvingly for recognizing that history was always a process of becoming, in the achievement of increasing self-consciousness. All static formulations of being, Childe argued, were committing the cardinal error of subsuming history to general laws rather than developing abstractions to render historical process more intelligible. To accept history as a creative process admitted that it was not subject to any external laws imposed from without. If history had order, it was not externally determined either biologically or theologically – nor was it teleological – instead the emergence of contemporary thought from prehistory obeyed an internal cultural logic: the triumph of reason.

Currently unfashionable and accused by postmodernists as totalitarian thought, the triumph of reason was for Childe, just as for Marx and Hegel, the culmination of Enlightenment thought. Moreover, it happened in Europe and archaeology had a rôle to play in unravelling the story. In 1947 no doubt one had every reason to think positively about the human condition. Fascism had been defeated and the future political stagnation of the Cold War was not yet obvious. Childe was a moral and ethical being who genuinely believed in human progress and thought archaeology helped chart the process by which the obstacles towards a more just and rational society had been overcome. No doubt in 1947, Childe had every reason to feel optimistic; hopes for a new social order based on redistributive justice were as high in Britain then as they are remote now.

I do not mean to defend Childe's account of the inventions and discoveries from the Old Stone Age onwards as a record of this triumph of reason in the West. In a brilliant article, Andrew Sherratt (1989) has ably demonstrated the strands of thought of the Enlightenment and the Romantic Movement that were jumbled up in Childe's personal view of development of the human condition. But does his particular view of the evidence available to him in 1947 make Childe some 19th-century dinosaur who could only think about the development of reason as stages of social advancement determined by changes in successive modes of production? Are we to dismiss the whole venture as archaeologically unsustainable, assuming this should be the sole arbiter of what informs archaeological practice? To ignore the ethical and moral imperatives behind Childe's personal interpretation of the past and to judge it on epistemological or empirical grounds alone would be, in my opinion, not only inadequate but to be part of the kind of cynicism that he fled from when he left behind the politics of the Australian Labor Party.

Let me remind you of Professor Mulvaney's quotation from Childe's conclusion to *How Labour governs* (1964(1923): 181):

> The Labor Party, starting with a band of inspired Socialists degenerated into a vast machine for capturing political power, but did not know how to use that power . . . except for the profit of individuals. . Such is the history of all labour organizations in Australia, and that is not because they are Australian, but because they are Labor. (Mulvaney 1978: 36)

Here in other words is a man for whom his academic writing matters because he thinks he can detect ethical and moral imperatives in the working of historical processes. The invisible hand of history, that Childe was fond of talking about, lay behind and gave order to personal machinations, opportunisms and the accidents of history. The version he particularly liked to quote was actually from a letter by Engels rather than Marx's better known passage from the 18th Brumaire of Louis Napoleon – for the good reason that it put faith in the idea that human action finally was shaped by something more than free will:

Men make their own history but not yet with a common will nor according to a collective plan, nor even in a deliberately planned society. Their efforts clash, and for that very reason all such societies are governed by necessity which appears under the form of accident. (Engels in Marx 1934)

This, one could say, is a familiar pattern of the intellectual figure desperately desiring to be relevant and engaged in the political game. Yet, burned by political hypocrisy and lack of idealism, Childe retreats into academe and convinces himself that, like patience on a monument, only he can see the historical process that will eventually create an order out of a chaos of personal ambitions and power politics.

Jurgen Habermas, probably the most influential sociological theorist of the postwar period, has defended the development of reason as the identity of modernity against the nihilistic philosophies of post-structuralism and post-modernism (Habermas 1987). The arguments are more subtle and expressively mediated than Childe's more provocative beliefs in inevitable human progress towards a state of absolute knowledge, but the implications for human action are the same.

As is well known, Childe's explanation for the development of reason as a core cultural value in the West was projected back deep into prehistory, in particular to the Bronze Age and the development of metallurgy. A superstitious and magic-ridden Neolithic world was superseded, he claimed, by a rationalist Bronze Age dedicated to the development of science untrammelled by orientalist despots or superstitious practices. Over the years since his death, much of his vision of the origins of the uniqueness of the West has been swept into the archaeological dustbin, in large part due to the endeavours of some colleagues who are here today.

But again, just as one stands poised with the archaeological dustpan and brush, the moral imperative, which can still lie behind the constitution of bad facts, comes whispering through.

Take Childe's description of the introduction of metallurgy in Europe in its most extreme orientalist version in *What happened in history (1942)*. Empirically it is all quite absurd, and conceptually it is clearly not up to modern rigorous standards. And yet why do I have this feeling that whether this adequately accounts for the origins of bronze metallurgy in Europe is the least important question to ask? Of course it does not explain it. But the description is not diffusionist in the classic orientalist sense of a creative centre irradiating a passive periphery. Instead it obeys the logic of Hegelian dialectics in the resolution of opposites. Metallurgy originates from the outside but is appropriated and recontextualized in a manner that gives the new technology entirely different social implications. In a classic version of

Marxist ontology, the freedom of European Bronze Age smiths to seek work and outlets for their products free from political constraint inverts the social conditions of production in oriental despotism and patronage by court elites. By representing Greek metics and Medieval wayfarers and journeyman as the heirs of Bronze Age smiths, a grand sociological history of freedom is concocted by Childe. Why Western society came to believe in freedom as a core value and why this arose only in Western society was rooted in the circumstances of innovation in production. This was scarcely first thought about by Childe, but he was the first to claim that prehistory held the answer. For Childe, as for his mentor Hegel, the purpose of history lay in creating the conditions for the achievement of absolute knowledge, which he detects as burgeoning in Europe in the Bronze Age with the emergence of freedom of production from political constraint. How on earth did this big idea get reduced to how metallurgy originated, an answer to which has required the development of a whole subdiscipline of archaeometallurgy? Somehow the fact that so much effort has been expended in proving Childe's vision wrong, as if the origins of metallurgy as a technical act was the real question, is an indictment of archaeological intellectual philistinism.

It is this ethical/moral Gordon Childe – the poser of questions about human freedom and responsibility to be answered by archaeology – that I want to pay homage to and finally to realize what he meant by saying:

My whole account may prove to be erroneous, my formulae may be inadequate . . . but I believe the attempt will still have been worthwhile. (Childe 1958: 74)

The rise of the West

It is precisely the ethics of Childe that I not only wish to celebrate but also to criticize because of some of their implications for the way we see the world now. Almost the whole of Childe's academic career was devoted to documenting "the prehistory of the rise of the West": how the triumph of reason had evolved through various vicissitudes in Europe and from there had spread throughout the world.

In that sense he was motivated by his 19th-century mentors Hegel and Marx in framing the uniqueness of Europe as the key world historical problem. It is true that he did not explore the roots of this universalist thesis in French and German nationalisms: the tangle between the French Enlightenment and the German Romantic Movement that produced a jumble of *Volksgeist* and techno-economic rationalism, or the contradictory belief that, although in some way cultures are like living beings and have their roots in the collective identity of the people, the form they take will obey some materialist logic of the transformation of productive forces. But then we are still trying to square that particular intellectual circle.

As an abstract intellectual problem it is probably impossible to solve, but we can at least take cognizance of the historical roots and recognize that we are concerned here with ideology and especially with the significance of the interaction between two modern ideologies: the rationalism and individualism of the Enlightenment, disseminated by the French Revolution, and the ideas and values which diverged from those of the West in Germany between 1770 and 1830. Louis Dumont (1986) has detected two phases in the dissemination and hybridization of these two national traditions.

Soon after the events of 1792, the ideals of the French Revolution became dominant in Europe. The three students who planted a tree of liberty in Tübingen, were Holderlin, Hegel and Schelling. In St Petersburg, young aristocrats converted to liberalism and conspired against the Czar. Yet this wholesale endorsement of French Revolutionary zeal rapidly diminished and an alternative intellectual and artistic blossoming established German culture, letters, and especially philosophy, on a new footing. At the same time it marked a process of estrangement between Germany and its western neighbours, as if the initial experience of acculturation dictated a path that a German identity could not follow without destroying itself. This gradual withdrawal of German cultural identity from the ideals of a rationally ordered and planned society in favour of culture – which so baffled contemporary observers – was explained by Ernst Troelstch in 1916 by the simple observation that the German lives in a community (*Gemeinschaft*) with which s/he identifies (Dumont 1986: 589). The ideal of living in a community, that survived into modern times in Germany, he argued was accompanied by feelings of belonging that subsumed all personal aspirations. The legitimacy of social and political authorities was also vested in quasi-mystical notions of leadership, rather than the social contract that lay at the root of the Enlightenment ideal of the relationship between the individual and the state. Of course, what developed into an ethnic theory of the nation was not limited to German thought and it became widely disseminated in eastern Europe, and particularly Russia, by the 19th century. Yet – and this is Dumont's main thesis – although German intellectual life privileged culture over society and holistic feelings over rational social engineering, it also favoured the development of individualism, the famous ideal of *Bildung* or "self-cultivation" so important in German literature from Goethe to Thomas Mann.

This combination of ethnic holism and individualism would remain incomprehensible, Dumont argues, were it not that the origin of this disposition lay much earlier with Luther and the German Reformation (Dumont 1986: 590). In the spread of Pietism, Luther asserted the cultivation of individualism as a religious duty in developing the relationship between a person and her/his God. This apparent paradox between ethnic holism and self-cultivating individualism provided the basis for German cultural resistance to the dominance of French culture up to and including the effects of the Revolution. Developed as a synthesis between holism and individualism, in particular by Hegel, it was as if the problems of modernity had been solved in the mind in Germany, whereas elsewhere it had to be resolved as a matter of political economy.

Archaicism was a particular feature of this German adaptation to modernity, as part of its claim to have modernized while remaining culturally intact. The success of an ethnic theory of the nation over a secular territorial theory of the state was even more widespread in Russia, where the reading of successive waves of German philosophers encouraged a convergence of view on culture history which remarkably is still the case in much archaeological practice in Germany and Russia. The idea that cultures are living beings, which form communities that have their roots in the collective identity of the people, developed into various forms of regional tradition in archaeology. A search for legendary origins to justify attaching a sense of community to a territorial state was also part of the archaicizing of culture. Familiar stories of idealized founding peoples, of the legendary origins of nations and peoples, of Ancient Teutons as staunch individualists, rationalized by Marx as the Germanic mode of production, served this purpose. Cultural singularity simply required a claim to a unique origin in a sense of place and time, embodying purity of essence. From this moral high ground as possessors of pure culture, the invention by others of modern syncretic states based on territorial sovereignty was all that remained for cultural hybrids such as the French and the English, whose miscegenated populations could lay claims to only imperfect histories.

The fateful implications of this substitution of race for state or nation has, of course, not been lost on most external observers and can be regarded as some kind of historical aberration now safely transcended. But the modern ideologies of the West that were a part of this debate were shaped by it in their espousal of the dominant values of uniqueness and singularity, of historical essentialisms and traditions and an aversion to cultural hybridization. In particular our whole language of culture and culture change has been transmitted through this filter of cultural authenticity and unique origins. Childe's Marxism was heavily imbued with it, as is all the language of culture contact, acculturation and change in neo-evolutionary theory.

Creolization and cultural origins

It can be argued that a belief in "Western civilization" rests on the fantasy of the existence of natural cultures which, through contact and acculturation, risk hybridization and loss of a sense of core value, e.g. freedom. This basic idea originated in Germany in the 18th century as a means of avoiding subsumption to the dominating ideas of the French Enlightenment, and through the Romantic Movement it became a powerful counter-force to its rival core value: the superiority of reason. The anthropologist Louis Dumont has detected a similar process of resistance and inversion of dominant values in the elaboration of caste in India as a reaction to British imperial rule (Dumont 1970), and Martin Bernal's interpretation of the rise of the Aryan model of Greek civilization as an 18th-century origin-myth has much merit (Bernal 1987); and the rapprochement between Childe's diffusionism and Bernal's hybrid model of Egyptian, Semitic and Greek origins of Western civilization is scarcely coincidental. That Bernal should find Childe's advocacy of *ex oriente lux* diffusionism an ethically respectable forerunner to his own argument is made even more comprehensible when one realizes that Bernal's father was J. D. Bernal, the British biochemist and Marxist whose four-volume *Science in history* (1964) movingly argued for the superior rationality of a science freed from the chains of capitalism.

Is it possible to move away from these assumptions about cultural origins and "purity". I would like to suggest that developments in linguistics, once a bastion of conservative thought, are worth considering. In the 19th century, an analogous obsession with natural units existed in linguistics. The question of what laws determine the origins of language, govern their growth and nec-essitate their decay dominated the study of language. None of these questions was solved by 19th-century philology, and, subsequent to the paradigm shift initiated by Saussure (1983), other questions came to be regarded as more important and more likely to have determinate answers. The solutions arrived at were taken over by those who continued to engage in philological inquiry, with rather dire consequences for philology. Inappropriate static entities were misused for describing dynamic processes and gaps in the descriptive accounts of idealized synchronic systems were accepted as causes of linguistic change. This is why, in the Chomskian structuralist framework of language and lin-guistics, it became important to remove such conjectural accounts of linguistic origins by removing altogether the question of language change as an histor-ical process. The basic assumption of the existence of synchronic entities whose origins could be investigated became quite erroneous.

The development of studies in Creole and pidgin languages has, however, begun to change all this. As in culture studies, Creole studies in linguistics have in the past suffered from the same bias against what were conceived to be hybridized versions of civilized European tongues. Many of the early accounts of pidgin and Creole languages were written by travellers and administrators to amuse others with stories about the ridiculous attempts by "natives" to speak their language. This bias towards what happens when natural language units come in contact with each other is currently opposed by the growing view that, in origin, all languages are hybrid.

Muhlhausler, one of the major writers on Creole languages, has recently asserted that:

> Language is not just for communicating with speakers of the same linguistic background but in the vast majority of cultures, bi- and multi-lingualism, dual lingualism, pidginization and similar phenomena are

crucially important and highly influential agents of change. Accommodation to speakers of other languages is probably more important in the history of language than internal processes. (Muhlhausler 1986)

What does this imply? That there exist only natural languages derived from single ancestral stocks? That we still work with the conceptual apparatuses of glottochronology and modern variants as analogues between language change and culture change?

Muhlhausler is arguing the reverse: that in origin there were only Creole languages with multiple ancestries which only very much later became natural languages when external power relations permitted standardization to be imposed. This account of language origins – i.e. from Creole to standard languages – is by no means generally accepted, but even a more conservative linguist such as Hall feels able to frame the basic question posed by pidgin and Creole languages as:

How far can structural borrowings go before they affect our classification of language? Can structural borrowings submerge the inherited system so thoroughly that later inspection cannot accept the actual "genetic" affiliation of the language? Is it possible for such borrowings to result in a language that actually has many "ancestors" rather than one. (Hall 1966: 117)

For Hall, such questions had not arisen previously in linguistics, because it was assumed that genetic relations were pure, that a given language could be related to one and only one language family. A current disposition apparently is to reject such notions of linguistic purity in favour of the view that all languages are mixed. In principle, Hall even acknowledges the possibility that a language might have existed where a perfect balance of hybridity made classification impossible.

The recognition of life-cycles in Creole languages and their absence in natural languages is another significant contrast that informs my argument. Hall explains the absence of life-cycles in "normal" languages because a language is not an organism but a set of habits handed down from one generation of speakers to another. The development from pidgin to Creole languages, on the other hand, represents an increase in complexity in the initial phase of reduction and simplification as contact languages are converted into standard languages of speech communities. Encountering language history as a truly dynamic process seems to lead us in the reverse of the expected order: we move from hybridity/creativity to standardization and habitual form in language development. It suggests that pidginization and creolization have been important stages in the life-cycles of many "natural languages" and Bickerton, in particular, has argued that any language can be understood only as part of an endless continuum (Bickerton 1975, 1976). A sense of the homogenous, for example the English language or culture, is in fact made up of heterogenous gradations extending from the familiar to the unfamiliar depending on the actor's own stance.

The assertion that both language and culture start in diversity, and become bounded only by agreement as to what constitutes a particular language or culture, corresponds with some recent theorizing on the way certain forms of modern ethnicity and cultural expression have developed. Hannerz, for example, asserts that there are no longer and perhaps never have been incommensurable cultures that have difficulty translating each other; instead there exists only a world culture created through increasing interconnectedness which he characterizes as the organization of diversity (1992: 208) and which may work towards either homogeneity or heterogeneity. Bickerton argues that language acquisition should originate in diversity and develop towards homogenization only under certain conditions. If there are no "natural languages", then by an analogue he draws with the socialization of children into language, he denies "natural cultures" except as some temporary closure around a consensus that may not in fact be mutually comprehensible to all its members.

This conclusion should be very exciting for archaeologists of a Childean persuasion, because it aids criticism of much received wisdom about the purity of natural cultures and other such essentialist notions on which identity is supposed to be built. The current trend in archaeology towards regional and inter-regional studies, which make no assumptions about bounded units or significant spatial patterns, is clearly part of this reaction, but the questioning of cultures as natural units should highlight some more specific theoretical questions. Childe's rendition of diffusionism in Hegelian terms bears many parallels to these contemporary debates about hybridization, since his argument about "culture change" hinged on the mechanism by which innovations were appropriated rather than culture contact per se. The difference of view is more than semantic; it is fundamentally about the concept of culture that he employed.

Hybrid origins and the archaeology of difference

Where then, between 19th-century ideologies of primordial cultures and late 20th-century Creole cultures (in their origin all things are hybrid, homogeneous "cultures" are a later product of political closure, ethnic cleansing, etc.), do we situate a re-working of Childe's historical approach? In particular, what was so significant about his reworking of 19th-century notions of diffusion, a reworking so radical that it was inappropriately described by his continued use of the term diffusion.

It is well known that Childe's particular brand of diffusionism was motivated by a wish to counteract the rise of racism and nationalism in archaeology and to absolve his own guilt over his previous adherence to the Aryan hypothesis. The force of his argument is just as pertinent today in archaeology, for example in eastern Europe where the legacy of the Romantic

Movement in archaeological practice has already conspired with current ethnic tensions to produce fateful consequences. Archaeology has been used by politicians in Serbia, Croatia and Macedonia to justify and resist territorial ambitions through claims of prior origin, and there is every likelihood that such misuse of archaeology will increase, for example in Georgia, where evidence of ancient Armenian settlement is currently being destroyed.

Although such individual acts are rightly condemned, archaeologists are often the first to celebrate building justifiable pride in a specific cultural tradition. Many archaeologists also today recognize the importance of regional traditions as a means of structuring research, often within individual countries. It is part of a reaction against generalizing goals and comparison in the subject and it is linked to post-processualist claims to multiple readings of the past and, at the extreme, to the relativist claim that one reading of the past is as good as another. The fact is that claims to primordial origins can be and are used to justify ownership of land that an ethnic group or state claims to have held from "time immemorial" or to adopt policies of domination and expansion over neighbouring peoples. The renaming or suppression of archaeological cultures and the redrawing of maps and boundaries in prehistory are all too familiar strategies.

Unfortunately this situation is no recent phenomenon in Europe, and the language and cultural categories are ready to hand for political misuse. A notable example of such misuse is the work of the 19th-century philologist and historian, Ernest Renan, the founder of Semitic philology, whose research was of crucial importance for the development of Semitic studies in general and Phoenician studies in particular.[1]

In a lecture published in 1862, entitled "The part played by Semitic peoples in the history of civilization", Renan summed up his findings in the following manner:

> The future, gentlemen, is for Europe alone. Europe will conquer the world and spread its religion which is law, freedom and respect for mankind, the belief that there is something divine at the heart of humanity. In all areas, progress for Indo-European peoples will consist in distancing themselves more and more from the Semite spirit . . .

and further

> . . . Islam is the complete negation of Europe. . . . it is the ghastly simplicity of the Semitic spirit, shrinking the brain and closing it to all delicate ideas, fine feelings and rational investigation, only to confront it with the eternal tautology – God is God. (Renan 1862)

One may well ask why ever did Renan become a Semitic scholar, and the answer is a systematic commitment to inquiry into the uniqueness of Europe through studying its Other. In this he was eminently successful. Ninety years later, Henri Frankfort, influenced by his reading of Levy-Bruhl (1922), would distinguish the rationality of the Greeks from the mythopoeic thought of the Ancient Egyptians, Semites and Modern Savages (Frankfort 1946: 3–27).

The principal result, particularly once the extreme orientalist attitudes of Renan and others were recognized for their racist implications, was the gradual marginalization of the Phoenicians as a worthy "object of study". The "otherness" of the Phoenicians (i.e. Jews) was retained in archaeological practice, but now shorn of any language that might have embarrassing connotations of anti-semitism. Instead, it is their lack of a contribution to Western Civilization, in contrast to the Greeks, that is emphasized. And what remains particularly significant is the rarity of Phoenician studies in archaeology. The context in which they could be studied becomes ambiguous and is made more difficult by the political conditions that have made archaeological study of the homeland sites in Palestine impossible in recent years. Archaeology stands convicted of developing a descriptive language in order to exclude the necessity or the embarrassment of considering certain kinds of questions and their effects on interpretations.

This is consistent with Martin Bernal's arguments (1987) about the involvement of archaeology in systematically ignoring evidence for Egyptianizing-Semitic contributions to Western civilization. One of the cornerstones of our account of later European prehistory has been the creation of a unified Mediterranean world through Greek and Phoenician colonization in the 8th and 7th centuries BC. However, the rôle of each apparent ethnic group has never been deemed equal. Phoenician colonization failed, while the Greek colonies disseminated literacy, science and philosophy, an interpretation that is part of the very myth of how the torch of freedom was transmitted to the West. Whatever the rationality of the archaeological evidence, a consistent subtext emerges. The Phoenicians were syncretist, hopeless muddlers and minglers of influences from all sorts of origins. A description of a Phoenician pidgin culture that never quite made it combines with baleful remarks about child sacrifice and the superficiality of a colonizing venture concerned only with commerce and trade. The Greeks on the other hand possessed an authentic and unified culture that although open to external influences was never subsumed by them.

This version of the "Great Divide" has never been supported by archaeological evidence. Archaeologically, if the Aegean was an outer periphery at the beginning of the colonization phase, it is cultural hybridity that distinguishes the material culture. At Lefkandi, the material culture has been identified as Euboean, Attic, Egyptianizing, Cypriot and Phoenician (Frankenstein, in press). The earliest foundation deposit at the Euboean colony of Pithecusae contains Euboean, Phoenician and Etruscan pottery, Phoenician or North Syrian seals, and faience of either Egyptian or Phoenician origin, the burial practice is not typically Aegean, and the children's graves contain seals of North Syrian or Levantine origin. One can enumerate other examples, but the pattern is clear: there is no Great Divide; it is even unclear whether the names Hellene/Greek or Phoenician mean anything in ethnic terms at this time. What is most striking is that this systematic creolization of material culture is rooted in the spread of ritual cults, the spread of seals and amulets, and new ideas about protection from misfortune. Walter Burkert has argued (1983) that the fear of pollution and the need for purification rise remarkably at the transition to the Archaic period in the Aegean. He cites the example of the city of Athens calling for purification for blood guilt, with Epimenides from Crete performing the task. He draws parallels between Assyrian incantation rituals and Greek magical thought at this time and claims that both are concerned with purification of the possessed person by incantation, sacrifice and the removal of polluting substances. One of the most striking features of burial rites is the importance attached to the expression and resolution of pollution associated with death. Sourvinou-Inwood (1991) contrasts the Homeric belief that everybody must die and go to Hades with the shift in attitudes in the 8th and 7th centuries to concern with purification of the body of both the living and the dead. Hence the elements in material culture that have been described as muddled Phoenician–Egyptianizing in derivation, are those that deal with sources of protective charms, magical spells, incantations and formulaic recitations which also express tensions between recitation and formulaic incantation in the spread of literacy and cult. And the potency in cult for the removal of polluting substances derives from materials of diverse origin that can be synthesized through cult activity into more powerful, protective statements.

Is this what colonization was all about, as later, with the spread of Islam, religion and trade were inseparable?. In this light, do corresponding changes in funerary cults in central and northern Europe during the early first millennium BC suggest the spread of a ritual concern with pollution removal in the preparation of the body and the spread of cremation rites. Could the frequency of razors and tweezers for hair removal in late Urnfield burials and Montelius period IV also suggest that a new ritualized association between masculinity, sexuality and pollution removal in funeral cults was not confined to the Mediterranean and that, a thousand years before the spread of Christian cults, cult and funerary practices of Semitic–Egyptian–Greek syncretist origins had spread throughout much of Europe?

It is ironic of course that, just as the West may be looking at its hybridized past as something of a virtue rather than a blight, the export of the concept of pure culture, through colonial administration, anthropology and development aid, is now beginning to acquire catastrophic proportions in the Third World. Nationalist and ethnic tensions, for example, are spreading in sub-Saharan Africa, where there has been a struggle to establish separate identity based on pride in cultural heritage but where the unintended consequences of the privileging of tradition has resulted in ethnic violence and massacre, first in South Africa and now elsewhere.

Consider the fact that only since 1960 has it been possible to envisage writing a history of Africa, and the writing of history by and for Africans is of even more recent date. A key issue that has emerged is the stance some

African historians and archaeologists have taken on the nature and origin of Ancient Egyptian civilization, asking whether it was continuous with or essentially different from that of sub-Saharan Africa. The recently published two volume UNESCO *General history of Africa* (1992) expresses the tension in the number of footnotes and addenda by editors disclaiming any responsibility for some of its contents. Volume 1 in particular stems from an innocuous sounding conference held in 1974, called "The peopling of Ancient Egypt and the deciphering of the Meroitic script". Ominous signs of a fractured text appear in the first paragraph of the Introduction where the editor reports that "discussion often took the form of successive and mutually contradictory monologues". It probably was not helped by the fact that the original conference was attended by ten Europeans, one American, one Sudanese, six Egyptians and only two Africans, one of whom was Cheikh Anta Diop, a strong believer in the argument for African origins of Egyptian civilization and hence of Western civilization in general. A heady brew!

Greenberg obviously didn't know what hit him in his chapter on African linguistics in volume 1 (UNESCO 1992). His association of Ancient Egyptian with Semitic languages rather than with Niger–Congo (i.e. Western Sudanic languages) raises Diop's ire, who manages to have a footnote attached to the chapter indicating that the conference had rejected Greenberg's findings. The Egyptian editor then adds a footnote to Diop's chapter referring to the controversial reception it received at the conference, adding tartly that all six Egyptians at the conference had positively refused to accept that they were Black.

At the root of the controversy is the fact that Diop claims to use the same sort of evidence and criteria for arguing for an African origin of Egyptian civilization as generations of Egyptologists have used, in his eyes, to ignore negroid features among Ancient Egyptians, in order to claim Egyptian civilization as a "White achievement'. He claims to be simply reversing the bias. In one of his wilder versions of the story of African origins, called *The cultural unity of Black Africa* (Diop 1960), world culture is described as derived from two original civilizations, one Northern and the other Southern, the former based on pastoralism, patrilineal descent, cremation rites and fire worship, and the latter on agriculture, matriliny, matriarchy, inhumed burial and divine kingship. This 19th-century style scrap-book of miscellaneous details may seem to many to be on the lunatic fringe. Yet the reception of Diop on Black campuses in the United States is little short of adulation, and Egyptology is one of the fastest growing subject areas in Black studies in the United States. In general, adherence to Diop is unequivocal, and any criticism of his facts is dismissed by many in Black studies as an obsession with details, indicative of how 150 years of "scientific objectivity" legitimized cultural thefts and historical fictions directly damaging to Black people. In a somewhat more moderate tone, in a recent book on Black Afro-American history, the highly respected Black Afro-American historian St Clair Drake (1987) deplores the polarization of views and the assembling of facts to assert racist positions and looks forward to the day when such activities will no longer be necessary.

What does seem clear is that the possibility of avoiding bias by claiming to be able to "tell things as they really are" will no longer do as a response, because the criteria normally used to evaluate evidence forbids it. This is part of a more general crisis in the production of intellectual work in the late 20th century, and certainly one product of this has been an increasing scepticism of academic claims to impersonal knowledge supported as objective truths that does not take account of the social context to which they belong. But I wish to argue that Childe's particular version of cultural origins in hybridity presents us with an alternative solution. Superficially Diop's pan-diffusionism would seem to invalidate any return to a Childean type of argument. Diop is clearly motivated by Western derived assumptions that Black and White cultures exist as natural cultural units which are involved in a struggle over which contributed most to something called "Western civilization". Developed in a more sophisticated manner, this is also the thesis of Martin Bernal's *Black Athena* (Bernal 1987). He argues that both the Egyptian (i.e. Black) and Phoenician (i.e. Semitic) contributions to Western civilization have been deliberately ignored in order to preserve progress for a White culture. Why everyone apparently wants to have played a rôle in the development of Western civilization is depressingly reductionist but nevertheless understandable, given that it does form the longest established view of world history so far expounded. Perhaps now we can recognize that this achievement is not a singular "European" effort but a well constructed product of hybrid origin and that it forms only a position on a cultural continuum of heterogeneity that invalidates such bounded notions as "the West", "Europe", "Islam", "Africa" as natural units founded in primordial origins.

Conclusion

Childe's refusal of racist theories and of fascism in the 1930s formed the ethical basis for his espousal of diffusionism. It is this moral imperative that separates Childe's diffusionism from all its 19th-century forebears and also underlies his fierce rejection of Stalin's unilinear evolutionary scheme in his articles on anthropology and archaeology (1946) and on *Archaeology as a social science* (1947b). Childe was labouring against the idea that cultural progress could be measured by the achievements of a single people. Cultural progress had resulted from breaking down the isolation of human groups and pooling their ideas on an ever-increasing scale. Egypt was the horror story of what happens when moribund social relations isolate a people from external contact – "Four centuries after the Iron Age had opened in Greece we find the Egyptian smith still using the clumsy tools of the Bronze Age" (Childe 1944: 23).

In contrast to classic diffusionist ideas, Childe emphasized the local appropriation of technical knowledges and ideas of external origin as a process by which the superiority of external origin was transcended. Whether it was the diffusion of writing from Phoenicia to Ancient Greece enabling science to rise in the latter rather than the former, or his negative views of what the Scots did with bronze metallurgy (they used it for trivial ornaments and to kill each other, rather than unleashing the productive forces) Childe stressed how the means and manner of appropriation of new knowledges determined "cultural achievement, thus criticizing the pan-diffusionist racial argument of active, dynamic centre acting upon a socially passive periphery. As I mentioned earlier, Childe had obviously read his Hegel on the dialectic and the growth of knowledge and, like Marx, saw himself turning Hegel on his head by showing that in "real prehistory" he could demonstrate in materialist terms what Hegel called *aufhebung* or sublation, the rising above or the transcendence of opposites. For Childe, culture in general had progressed by what he called the pooling of ideas as an active and practical process of cultural transcendence. I would argue that he initiated a theory of cultural process that has scarcely been developed in archaeology since, but, through borrowing the concept of creolization from linguistics, could be developed into a more radical approach to questions of origins which would have both ethical and intellectual imperatives.

Over 50 years ago Childe had realized the sterility and barrenness of the Romantic Movement's legacy of culture as natural units and had modified the concept of diffusion to argue that all cultures in their origin must be hybrid, and that hybridization is the stuff of creativity and dynamism through a dialectical resolution of opposites. Moreover, in contrast to some more modern writers, he was critically and passionately aware of the implications of what he was advocating and the rôle that archaeology had played and could play in the future. In what might be called the Latin American route to development, Childe stressed discontinuity instead of continuity, systematic breaks in cultural continua, and argued that mingled peoples increased the stock of ideas available and encouraged innovation and change.

I have argued that Gordon Childe's belief that the study of the past has to be liberating is still the most important and enduring legacy of his work in archaeology. It brings to the fore the potentially ethnocentric, if not racist, implications of apparently innocuous archaeological reasoning. It promotes critical self-reflection in a subject that is not well known for taking such issues seriously. Moreover it presents us still with clear ethical alternatives. What kinds of pasts do we want to emphasize in relation to what kinds of futures. To use a felicitous phrase of Paul Gilroy (pers. comm.), it encourages us to choose whether we wish to stress roots or routes in the forging of cultural identities.

1. I owe this section to Susan Frankenstein's analysis of Phoenician colonization in the western Mediterranean (in press).

References

Bernal, J. D. 1964. *Science in history*, 4 vols. London: Watts.

Bernal, M. 1987. *Black Athena: the Afroasiatic roots of Classical civilization*. London: Free Association Books.

Bickerton, D. 1975. *Dynamics of a Creole system* Cambridge: Cambridge University Press.

Bickerton, D. 1976. Pidgin and Creole studies. *Annual Review of Anthropology* **5**, 169–93.

Burkert, W. 1983. *Homo necans: the anthropology of ancient Greek sacrificial ritual and myth*. Berkeley: University of California Press.

Childe, V. G. 1942. *What happened in history*. Harmondsworth: Penguin.

Childe, V. G. 1944. Archaeological ages as technological stages.*Royal Anthropological Institute, Journal* **77**, 7–24.

Childe, V. G. 1946. Archaeology and anthropology. *Southwestern Journal of Anthropology* **2**, 243–51.

Childe, V. G. 1947a. *History*. London: Cobbett Press.

Childe, V. G. 1947b. Archaeology as a social science. *University of London Institute of Archaeology, Third Annual Report*: 49–60.

Childe, V. G. 1958. Retrospect. *Antiquity* **32**, 69–74.

Diop, C. A. 1959. *L'unité culturelle de l'Afrique noire*. Paris. (1960. *The cultural unity of Black Africa*. London.)

Diop, C. A. 1960. *L'Afrique noire pré-coloniale*. Paris: Presence Africaine.

Drake, St Clair 1987. *Black folk here and there: an essay in history and anthropology*. Los Angeles: University of California Press.

Dumont, L. 1970. *Homo hierarchicus*. London: Weidenfeld & Nicolson.

Dumont, L. 1986. Are cultures living beings? German identity in interaction. *Man* **21**, 587–605.

Frankenstein, S., in press. *The archaeology of colonialism*. Barcelona: Edita critica.

Frankfort, H. 1946. *The intellectual adventure of ancient man*. Chicago: Universiy of Chicago Press.

Habermas, J. 1987. *The philosophical discourse of modernity*. Cambridge: Polity.

Hall, R. A. 1966. *Pidgin and Creole languages*. Ithaca: Cornell University Press.

Hannerz, U. 1992. *Cultural complexity: studies in the social organisation of meaning*. New York: Columbia University Press.

Levy-Bruhl. L. 1922. *La mentalité primitive*. Paris: Alcan.

Marx, K. 1934. *The 18th Brumaire of Louis Napoleon*. Moscow: Progress Publishers.

Muhlhausler, P. 1986. *Pidgin and Creole linguistics*. Oxford: Basil Blackwell.

Mulvaney, J. D. 1978. Australia before the Europeans. *Bulletin of the Institute of Archaeology, University of London* **15**, 35–47.

Renan, E. 1862. *De l'origine de langage*. Paris: Michel Lévy.

Saussure, Ferdinand de 1983. *Course in general linguistics*. London: Duckworth.

Sherratt, A. 1989. V. Gordon Childe: archaeology and intellectual history. *Past and Present* **125**, 151–85.

Sourvinou-Inwood, C. 1991. *Reading Greek culture: texts and images, rituals and myths*. Oxford: Oxford University Press.

UNESCO 1992. *General history of Africa*, 2 vols. London: Macmillan.

Discussion
CHAIRED BY JOHN WILKES

Trigger: I have two comments, one very specific one on the Phoenician/ European distinction and one on the 19th-century's uses of the image of the Phoenicians. There is another aspect to the distinction, in which Greeks become a metaphor for the French, and Phoenicians become a metaphor for the English. Quite apart from the Oriental versus European battles, this set of identities was played out as a French critique of the English, and a lot of English writers accepted that distinction, that the Phoenicians, with their entrepreneurship and so on, were in fact analogous to the English. You even get people, like Harold Peake in the twentieth century, who said that one of the reasons the British were financially successful is because the biological descendants of the Phoenicians were still wandering around southern England, indeed working in the City stock exchange! But beyond this there is another point: that German prehistorians, no matter how far back they looked in their history, saw only Germans, and that encouraged in the 19th century the idea that the source of German greatness was their racial purity.

Secondly, if one considers 19th-century British historians, one finds that when they looked back, they saw the Normans, the Saxons, the Romans and several waves of Celtic peoples, and certainly for them the source of British greatness was hybrid vigour. It was albeit a White racist view, but all these ethnic groups were seen as having come together and somehow the best each had to offer had blended to make the British better than anybody else. So, in fact, when Childe is talking about diffusion and mixture, he is not only developing his own critique of Kossinna, he is also carrying on the myth that had started in British historiography in the 19th century, and was indeed part of the thinking of Myres and Evans, his mentors. I wonder therefore whether it is worth trying to find alien roots for something that is really so much more home-grown and homely and was available as part of the British historiographic tradition at this period.

Rowlands: Yes, obviously the context is nationalism and the various kinds of national ideologies, but I think it is wrong to assume that they developed separately from each other. My point is the way in which their mutual interaction, competition and antagonism was the ground on which ideas about vigour and hybridity versus purity were played out, and that the same language categories could be given different meanings and content in different situations within the same national tradition. But the overriding point is that it is the way in which national identities and nationalisms were not only generated but also developed as a means of overcoming these contradictions. This seems to be the broader question to try to understand: why in France this, why in Britain that, why in Germany something else? That is why I started off with the point about the reception of the French Revolution in Germany as relevant to an understanding of German ideologies, and particularly of German culture. I don't pretend that mine is in any way a sophisticated analysis, but it is the stress on the interaction of nationalisms rather than seeing them just as independent entities, which then simply stand opposed to each other, that I was trying to get at.

Wilkes: It is interesting here to contemplate different national views of historically identified figures who resisted the Romans. The Germans clearly identified with Hermann/Arminius as a figure of resistance. In the case of France, it seems that there was some confusion as to whether they were really on the side of Vercingetorix, the great resister, or perhaps, and this was certainly the case with Napoleon III, they were on the side of Julius Caesar. Whereas the British view of our great resistance heroes was distinctly different. In the 18th century, in William Cowper's poem on Boadicea (Boudicca), her descendants will one day become rulers of the world, which the Caesars could never dream of being. By the end of the 19th century, that view has changed, in that a standard work on ancient history, which concluded with a description of the rebellion of Boudicca, contains the phrase: "We, the English, know how the Romans felt at the moment when destruction occurred, because of how it felt in India at the time of the Mutiny". These views seem not only to have changed but also to have been the subject of manipulation, for, in the case of Boudicca, she is now not *of* England, only in it, and the Roman conquest is seen as part of a formative stage which gave the English their particular character.

Renfrew: I am intrigued by your advocacy of hybridization in the linguistic field for the origin of language families because I, too, have found this attractive, but have been much less successful than you in finding linguistic authorities who support the concept. If I could identify some linguistic authorities who would say "yes" to the idea that pidgin/Creole is really the heart of language formation, I would be tempted to support that view, but I have to say that in all the reading I have undertaken I have never found any historical linguist – not even Creole specialists such as Thomason and Kaufman – who regards *any* language, other than the Creoles and pidgin of the 20th, 19th and 18th centuries, as, in any meaningful sense, a hybrid language. Every linguist I can find says "no, if you take any language, it has *an* ancestor, not several ancestors". And if you ever mention to them Trubetskoy – the Russian linguist who toyed with the notion that the Indo-European languages might have emerged by a process of convergence and fusion – it is enough just to mention the word "Trubetskoy" to any historical linguists and you will immediately unify them against the idea. Your view does not match with my perception of the general view in the field of historical linguistics, but that still might allow that you are right and they are wrong.

Rowlands: Well, I can always claim that there are possibilities of openness there, because the linguists seemed to react to you in such an emotional manner. Whenever anyone reacts emotionally to mention of this simple idea, then I suspect that there is something more going on than the apparent facts of the situation. I think there is enough in the idea to justify investigating it a bit further, particularly if one moves outside the classic field of historical linguistics and Indo-European studies into studies of Creole and pidgin languages in Africa and Oceania. There does seem to be more open-mindedness there, at least in terms of how I read the linguists. But I am quite willing to accept that I am on the thin end of the wedge at the moment, so let us hope that the emotional reaction to your mentioning Trubetskoy betrays at least some worry rather than pure and utter confidence.

Shennan: I think you made a very eloquent case, Mike, in arguing for a particular rôle for Childe in terms of his moral and ethical perspective, and his ideas about the relationship between the West and the East. It seems to me that if you look at his last book, *The prehistory of European society*, with its emphasis, as Bruce Trigger quoted, on the dynamics of European free enterprise and the contrast between this and the dead end of the Near East, it reflects precisely the kind of orientalist view that Renan represents and that you have been criticizing.

Rowlands: Yes, I think the point that Childe was making was of course that capitalism had emerged in Europe and nowhere else in the world and that, to progress, societies had to go through it. It is not that there is any irony in ending up in free enterprise. The whole point is that you have to go through capitalism in order to reach socialism, and therefore capitalism represents the highest stage of society so far achieved. And he gave his own, prehistorian's answer to the large historical problem of why Europe and nowhere else. But he did not escape the East/West dualism on which it was based, and after all he did die nearly 40 years ago and was unable to escape the orientalist underpinnings of that world view. Now we can look back retrospectively on how he was trying to recognize that something was wrong. I think there was a tension there and that he was aware that it was not simply a dualism between East and West which counterpoised in a bi-polar set of opposites. I think there is implicit in his work some idea of movement, of continua between those bi-polar opposites within that dualism. And that is what fascinates me, because here is a mind trying to escape from these categories, from which, obviously, he could not escape completely.

Hodson: May I get back to Childe's view of culture? Would you say that there is at any stage something which you can detect as an entity that you would give a name to, as either a language or an archaeological culture? This is interesting in relation to Childe's approach to cultures, and there is lot of controversy about this today, archaeologically.

Rowlands: Again, I think there is an ambiguity or paradox between the idea of cultures as natural units, in the same way that languages are regarded as natural units, and the fact that I was trying to detect – within the received idea of Childe's use of the culture concept – an attempt by him to introduce the idea that cultures were not naturally homogeneous, that in a sense they were constantly in creation; if they were units, that there was some notion of becoming, in terms of this process of hybridization, this taking in of ideas and materials of external origin and possessing them. Therefore there was a process which was not the same as the idea of an essentialist notion of cultures as natural units. But he could not escape from the idea of cultures as units, which, as you imply, archaeology has been concerned to refute.

Hodson: Would you recognize that there are such things as languages that you can give a name to, however they are formed and however they change?

Rowlands: Yes, I follow Muhlhausler's view that there are power languages, and when one talks about languages as units one refers to the conditions under which they become standardized. Muhlhausler uses the term "power language" to describe the conditions, often temporary, under which a language unit might be formed. Now that, I think, is a valuable idea in terms of looking at ethnogenesis, for example. That is what I am trying to get at.

References

Muhlhausler, P. 1986. *Pidgin and Creole linguistics.* Oxford: Basil Blackwell.
Thomason, S. H. & T. Kaufman 1988. *Language contact, creolization and genetic linguistics.* Berkeley: University of California Press.
Trubetzkoy, N. S. 1939. Gedanken über das Indogermanenproblem. *Acta Linguistica.* 1, 81–9.

"Another university man gone wrong"
V. Gordon Childe 1892–1922

JOHN MULVANEY

Working briefly as a public servant in the London office of the Agent-General for New South Wales in 1922, Gordon Childe turned 30 years of age the week before he was notified of the termination of his services. That action played a crucial part in reshaping his European career. Previously, however, except for Childe's three years at Oxford between 1914 and 1917, his formative life was centred on New South Wales and Queensland. His tempestuous Australian episode between 1917 and 1922 has been subjected to belated examination, particularly by Terry Irving, a Sydney political scientist, and by a Brisbane historian, Raymond Evans. Their findings, together with other stimulating insights into Australian cultural life during Childe's Australian years, were presented by participants in the Brisbane Childe Conference in October 1990 (Irving et al., in press)

Although the general perspective of Sally Green's excellent biography of Childe remains intact, various aspects of his Australian experience have been clarified since its publication in 1981. Childe's outstanding contribution to Australian political commentary, and the saga of the violation of his civil liberties, merit the attention which they are receiving. His first book, *How Labour governs* (1923), remains one of the rare trenchant studies of Australian politics. His searing experiences as a pacifist and socialist intellectual in wartime Australia must have played a vital rôle in shaping his psyche.

My concern is to build upon the research by Irving and Evans, and to present an insight into that intense citizen and political activist who was Gordon Childe, before he became transformed into the renowned expatriate prehistorian. Most British academics probably agree with Alison Ravetz (1959: 56) who judged Childe as "first and last a working archaeologist". That assessment ignores the first three decades of his life and overlooks his Australian identity, so often cited by himself to justify or to assert presumed eccentricities. Even Stuart Piggott's perceptive obituary assessment dismissed Childe's Australian years in one paragraph, and therefore treated Childe as essentially a prehistorian (Piggott 1958).

By coincidence, I also was aged 30 when I first moved from teaching history to practising prehistory. That experience convinces me how deeply one's life-way is set during three decades, and how inherited intellectual influences determine the shape of a newly directed career. I am neither attempting an excursion into parallel lives nor comparing chalk with cheese, but my own first researched publication was an article on the history of the Australian Labor Party. Unlike Childe, I found political history dull, although I am pleased to note that in that remote year of 1948, when Childe's writings on prehistory were virtually unknown to me, I praised *How Labour governs* as "a classic, which should be read by any supporter of Labour" (Mulvaney 1949: 45).

Elsewhere, I have recounted my brief contacts with Gordon Childe upon his return in 1957 from his self-imposed exile. My testimony is a tribute to his goodwill and good humour. Having never met me previously, he delivered two lectures to my ancient history class, the first at three hours' notice. He proved a cheerful companion on the day when, at his request, I drove him to the forested Dandenong Ranges, outside Melbourne, in a fruitless search for lyre-birds (Mulvaney 1990).

Prelude

Childe (1947: 5) instructed historians that, "It should be the historian's business to disclose an order in the process of human history". I intend to individualize that advice and trace an order in the process of Childe's Australian years. Gordon's childhood was spent chiefly in the scenic Blue Mountains, at Leura, some 60 miles west of Sydney and eight miles from Govett's Leap, where he died. His father, an Anglican rector in North Sydney, owned a house at Leura where, critics complained, he spent undue time.

Gordon was educated privately until he turned 15, so perforce, he was a solitary lad. He was enrolled at Sydney Church of England Boys Grammar School in 1907, one of Australia's premier private schools. His matriculation year in 1910 was saddened by his mother's death. She was his father's second wife and Gordon was her only surviving child. Thereafter he had little contact with his father who, like his two step-sisters and step-brother, strongly disapproved of his later political opinions.

Enrolment at the University of Sydney in 1911 was followed by graduation in 1914 with first class honours in Latin, Greek and philosophy, a University Medal and a philosophy prize. Fellow undergraduate Herbert Vere Evatt and Childe became close friends. Evatt studied law and eventually led the Australian Labor Party.

The calibre of Childe's leading teachers may have proved a major influence upon his approach to learning. His professor of Greek, W. J. Woodhouse (1866–1937), later advised him to enter for archaeology at Oxford. Woodhouse was an influential teacher who had a background in Greek topographic archaeological exploration during the 1890s. His biographer, L. F. Fitzhardinge (1990: 562), recalled characteristics which might have aptly described Childe:

Seldom sticking close to the text or appearing to notice his class, he conveyed his enthusiasm, critical approach and genial humanity in appalling rambling soliloquies seasoned with a chain of anecdotes and a puckish humour. It was impossible to take notes, but at the end of the year students found that they had acquired, almost unconsciously, much general wisdom and a fund of exact knowledge.

Childe was also fortunate in his philosophy mentor. (Sir) Francis Anderson (1858–1941), Challis Professor of Logic and Mental Philosophy, was an Hegelian "Christian Idealist" who explored the interconnections of disciplines, emphasized an historical approach to problems, and, unusual in that period, encouraged wide reading and non-conformist intellectual values; he even tolerated dissent and stimulated questions during class. Significantly, he also championed the Workers' Educational Association (WEA), with which Childe became closely associated (O'Neil 1979).

Anticipating later discussion, let us advance to 11 December 1918, in the context of Anderson's influence. Although this was a month since the Armistice, Australian military intelligence still supervised censorship. Childe's mail was being intercepted because he was classed as a dangerous radical. Evatt was then an associate of the NSW Chief Justice, although his political views were similar to Childe's. When the censor opened a letter which Evatt sent to Childe, he summarized its contents but was unable to identify its sender, because Evatt signed as "Bert". Evatt now condemned Anderson's philosophy courses as irrelevant liberal radicalism. He suggested that he and Childe should collaborate in writing a text "renouncing" bourgeois philosophy.[1] The disapproving censor noted, in his (so-called) intelligence report, that the writer "seems to be quite prepared to follow Childe blindly". Indeed, Childe and Evatt maintained a lifelong intellectual friendship.

Peter Gathercole is the authority on Childe's Oxford years, his political education and contacts. I simply emphasize that Childe disembarked in England in 1914 exceptionally well prepared in classical languages and logical mode of expression, and was unusually well read in radical political and social theory, including familiarity with Marx, Engels and Hegel.

New South Wales, 1917–18

Childe arrived back in Sydney around August 1917. Because he was known as a pacifist who made no secret of his strong anti-war and socialist sentiments, the intelligence service was alerted. Although he suffered many indignities and much injustice, the fact that neither he nor most of his associates were arrested or interned needs to be stated. Neither the enormous war casualties, nor government policies, fostered an atmosphere of dissent. While I make no attempt to justify reactionary treatment of sincere persons such as Childe, it is necessary to set their activities within their social context.

This was total war. Australia's percentage of casualties of those at the front was the highest in the British Empire. Voluntary recruitment within the population of five million people produced 416,000 enlistments; of this number, 210,000 became casualties, including more than 59,000 killed. Despite this tragically impressive record, the Labor Party government advocated compulsory military service to enlarge the armed forces. Constitutional requirements necessitated a referendum, which was held during October 1916. It was defeated, largely by Labor supporters, particularly those of Irish descent. The Prime Minister, W. M. Hughes, led many colleagues out of the Party and governed with Opposition support. An election in May 1917 returned the new National Party, a merger of the Hughes faction and the Liberal Party. Even so, when that government held a second conscription referendum in December 1917, it also was defeated.

Childe's return therefore coincided with a time of deep political emotion, verging on hysteria. The Hughes government regarded dissent as tantamount to treason, while Russia's Bolshevik revolution served to emphasize the menace of social disorder. Few Australians possessed either the knowledge or the inclination to distinguish between shades of red on the far political left; all versions of socialism were potentially Bolshevik.

Surveillance was conducted through Army intelligence officers in each capital city, under whom District Censors supervised postal and press censorship. (Some of these censors were former university staff, which possibly influenced them against troublesome "intellectuals".) Although the chain of intelligence command extended up to the Chief of the General Staff, both the Minister for Defence and the Prime Minister used the intelligence service without reference to its commander.

Hughes increased demands for surveillance of opponents "with little regard for whether they were moderates or extreme left-wingers". This list included all pacifist groups, the Society of Friends, many anti-conscription politicians, and the staff of the university-associated WEA. Childe was only one of several literate and public intellectuals who attracted particular attention. So did future Australian Labor Party leaders Evatt and Arthur Calwell (Cain 1983: ix–xi, 58–9, 130).

Fortunately for historians, mail written by or addressed to prominent malcontents was intercepted and summarized on official forms by the censors, to which they appended their pungent and outrageously biased political and moral observations. The Australian Archives are the repository, therefore, of much information concerning the life and times of V. Gordon Childe.

It is not surprising that in war-time Australia, when few families were spared the casualty list, it was poor solace to be told by anti-war propagandists that their dead or maimed kin were sacrifices to the capitalist cause. Worse still, the "Bolsheviks" quoted strange foreign names which sounded like enemy sources. Lay persons who read the bellicose but "pro-Australian" newspapers, or harkened to the Prime Minister (the "little Digger"), remained blissfully unaware that the war was an unjust one.

Assessed within this tragic setting, Childe's dedicated opposition to the war and his citation of European radical theorists, has a sense of unreality. What, for example, might the citizen of the rural Queensland town of Maryborough have made of Childe's dignified letter to the *Maryborough Chronicle*, on 29 November 1918? In defending his situation (discussed below), he referred to "the doctrines of Kropotkin and Bakunin!" of whose identity they would have been entirely unaware.

Presumably Childe's gilt-edged academic credentials ensured his appointment, late in 1917, as Senior Resident Tutor at St Andrew's College, on the campus of the University of Sydney. As H. V. Evatt was a resident tutor there at the time, he may have assisted the appointment. It is interesting that Raymond Dart was the college Vice-President and Senior Tutor in 1917. Before he departed on war service, his residence overlapped with Childe's, so he probably also advised on Childe's appointment. By Easter 1918, however, Childe's public pacifist and socialist activities became an embarrassment to the college authorities. At least they proved unacceptable to the university administration, which was urged on by the Intelligence Service. This unseemly episode has been described by Jim Allen (1981). Honourably accepting the inevitable, Childe offered to resign from 1 June 1918, and this was accepted with alacrity (Green 1981: 28–9), and Evatt succeeded him as Senior Tutor.

That St Andrew's staff deplored Childe's departure is indicated by an illuminating note in the 1918 number of the college magazine (St Andrew's 1918: 12):

> Mr Childe came to the College an entire stranger to us, and it speaks volumes for his personal worth that when he left us at the end of the first term he had won the respect and esteem of all the men. His scholarship was of the first order, and his tea and cigarettes were second to none. His pipe was a thing of beauty and a joy for ever. He did not seek to be popular; he just became so. Owing to the fact that in this as yet intolerant world, it is not possible at a time of crisis to hold social and political views contrary to those in the majority, it became desirable, in the interests of the College, that Mr Childe leave us. He took the only proper course in the situation - that of voluntarily resigning - to the great regret of all those who knew him.

His departure did not go unremarked in the State parliament where his case was raised for the first time as an issue of civil rights. The question posed by Labor member William McKell, a future Governor-General, was given a negative and evasive response.[2]

Seeking alternative employment, Childe turned to the Catholic College of St John's. Its Rector was the Reverend M. J. O'Reilly, an orator of note, an opponent of conscription and a prominent name on the Intelligence Service list. Evidently Childe had sought O'Reilly's assistance and he had written to thank him for his sympathy and expressions of goodwill, even though no position was available. The censor felt it was necessary to justify the failure to intercept O'Reilly's letter, for it indicated the limitations of postal surveillance. "Probably it was delivered by hand as the two colleges are within a couple of minutes of each other", he reported with some irritation.[3]

Childe had already written to a young medical graduate at Melbourne University, F. J. Williams, an anti-conscription activist. "I naturally would accept any sort of work available, he told Williams on 3 May 1918.[4] "Unfortunately" he continued, "I have no testimonials or references, and am not likely to get any, except it be from laborites or pacifists. For this reason I think that school work would be difficult if not absolutely impossible to obtain". The censor must have felt rewarded to copy Childe's enclosed *curriculum vitae*, as it recorded his secretaryship of the Oxford University Socialist Society, under the presidency of G. D. H. Cole. The communication incidentally alerted the censor to the extent of Williams's radical contacts. As a consequence, the Melbourne district censor warned the university Registrar concerning his activities (Cain 1983: 131).

Childe soon wrote again to Williams, informing him that employment in Queensland was a possibility, through the influence of both that State's Labor premier and the Treasurer.[5] Evidently, McKell interceded with them on Childe's behalf (Kelly 1971: 22). The censor quoted from Childe's letter with interest, "that the Pacifists section of the [NSW] Labor Council is very strong . . . Privately I am supplying information to them". "On the other hand", Childe regretted, "recruiting is horribly successful" Amongst the irate censor's acerbic comments were the following revealing judgements:

2. Childe is seeking a job in Queensland. Attention of Censor Brisbane is directed to this fact.

3. Childe here shows himself as a Pacifist of the deepest dye, and a supporter of Labor.

4. The University of Sydney should be well rid of him.

The pervading anti-intellectualism and conservative siege mentality which conditioned officialdom in the face of the presumed "red menace", is evident from cameo responses by censors to Childe's activities. During August 1918 he notified Mrs [Bertha] McNamara of a forthcoming public meeting. "Mrs McNamara seems to be becoming an intellectual" sneered the censor.[6] In fact, Bertha McNamara possessed intellect, learning and spirit. She was a redoubtable Polish-born socialist, feminist and bookshop proprietor, the shop being a meeting place for radicals. One of her daughters married J. T. Lang, a future premier, while another wed Henry Lawson, doyen of Australian bush writers.

That same month Childe wrote to Frederick Sinclaire, a former Unitarian minister, a member of the Victorian Socialist Party, secretary of the Fabian Society, and principal of the Victorian Labor College, a workers' educational institution independent of the university-controlled WEA.[7] Childe sought information about that college's structure, because he considered establishing a similar college in Sydney, with support from the trades unions. "Childe's suggestion . . . is noteworthy" observed the worried censor. Indeed, when such a college was announced for Sydney in 1919 (but not by Childe), it was modelled on the Melbourne concept. The worried censor's response was to warn against: "The growth of extreme doctrines and principles amongst the working class", resulting from "their heads filled with dangerous ideas" (Cain 1983: 128–9). Yet Sinclaire's notions were hardly the stuff of revolution. He simply was "a formidable exponent of essentially Edwardian literary socialism . . . combined with modernist theology" (Walker 1988: 616).

When Childe received a letter from an Oxford tutor, J. R. McGrath, the censor was pleased to note that he was unsympathetic to Childe's problems:[8] "I am sorry you don't get along better with the authorities. The fault in these cases is seldom wholly on one side". Stating his ignorance of Australian politics, McGrath however presumed an Australian desire to eliminate German influence in the South Pacific. Here was a potential gain for the acute censor: "an attempt will be made to intercept Childe's reply in order to obtain his views on the question of Germans in the Pacific".

During August 1918 Childe had applied for a tutorship in ancient history in the university-affiliated WEA (extra-mural adult education). The electoral committee consisting of WEA and university staff recommended Childe's appointment, but the university Senate did not appoint him, evidently acting under government pressure. This celebrated issue was examined by Green (1981: 29–31). Radical circles correctly interpreted this decision as a violation of academic and civil freedom. Labor members McKell and T. J. Smith raised the matter in Parliament, Smith speaking cogently and at length in Childe's support, but to no avail.[9]

Childe again turned for support to Father O'Reilly at St John's College,[10] informing him that, "in a rash moment of jingoism the Senate have . . . just rejected the recommendation . . . on the grounds of my alleged political opinions . . . I think it very desirable that the true facts should be published now". The censor approvingly remarked: "It is satisfactory to note that the Senate have [sic] been strong enough to take action on their own initiative, but it is safe to say that they would not state their ground as suggested by Childe".

Outspoken radicals from various camps rallied to Childe's cause. Sinclaire proved sympathetic but unhelpful in Melbourne. In the intelligence file associated with their correspondence, however, is a typed copy of a statement four paragraphs in length.[11] It traced the University of Sydney's comparable record in its treatment of a professor (G. A. Wood) who opposed the Boer War; it described the university Senate's adverse reaction when O'Reilly adopted a public stand against conscription. It then canvassed Childe's qualifications and his rejection because of his "unorthodox views on the war, having joined The Society of Friends, the ALP . . . and other bodies in a peace conference at Easter. He was also alleged to have used in a letter the words "I believe the war destructive of civilization and true liberty and must work for an immediate peace."

Probably the author of this document was William John Miles (1871–1942), a republican and secretary of the Rationalist Association. Miles, a wealthy Sydney accountant, at that time supported anti-war and socialist causes, but adopted neofascism during the 1930s. When writing to a Labor member of the Queensland State parliament, he raised the above issues in similar phraseology and order. Childe was about to leave for Brisbane and Miles sought support for him there. He also wrote, according to the censor, "in similar strain" to ten other Queensland radicals.[12] As Queensland had a Labor government, the censor deplored the likelihood that Childe's "undoubted ability combined with his extravagant tendencies will ensure for him a hearty reception".

Miles also sought assistance from a prominent Melbourne activist, Robert S. Ross, whom the censors pursued with "ferocity" as a particularly dangerous influence (Cain 1983: 130). Ross hesitated to write a public defence of Childe, however, as he wondered whether "we are at liberty to publish that. I wanted to mention this matter some time back but it was said that it would do Childe harm . . . Until I hear further from you I am holding back the paragraph". Ross could have published, because Childe was already damned.[13] A militant trade unionist and NSW parliamentarian, P. S. Brookfield, also chipped in to assist.[14] Writing to a Queensland State Member, he requested his support, because Childe was "a case of unadulterated victimization".

Queensland, 1918–19

In mid-September Childe therefore left for Brisbane full of optimism, preceded by a sheaf of enthusiastic introductions. His move caused consternation within the conservative Childe family, however, because Gordon's stepsisters and his half-brother lived in Queensland. Ethel lived in Toowoomba, while Alice Vernon, an Anglican nun, was in Townsville; Laurence was a Brisbane bank clerk. Alice attempted to divert Gordon to South Australia, writing twice when she heard of his possible intrusion into their territory (Evans, in press). Her second attempt combined pleading with panic, in the censor's summary:[15]

1. With regard to what you wrote about Brisbane, it would of course make all the difference if you could keep clear of politics . . .
2. But I don't think it would be good for you to live in this *little* city, holding a position from a Government to whom you have avowed yourself a friend and partisan and yet stand aloof. You would then become involved in politics – it would be inevitable sooner or later and that means a feud with brother Laurie. Your side is not his.
3. One thing is certain, that if you come here, you and Laurie will be alienated.

The censor's diligent reading and transcribing completed, he added with feeling: "It is a pity the writer cannot impart to him some of her commonsense and insight, and finer feelings . . . "

Even the best efforts of Childe's supporters failed to secure him a Brisbane post, not even William McKell who contacted the Treasurer, E. G. Theodore. Childe sought a teaching post in the State secondary school system, but he was informed that no vacancy existed.[16] For some time Childe received hospitality from George Pearce, a socialist high on the Intelligence list. Then he moved to the home of the eccentric Reverend T. C. Witherby, head of the local WEA. "Witherby has a long record in [intelligence] reports", noted the severe censor,[17] "showing him to be a man very similar to Childe, another university man gone wrong".

Young Jack Lindsay, the future prolific author, was on Witherby's staff and he, Witherby and Childe became friends. They spent unconventional weekends together on the forested Mt Tamborine, living in Witherby's rickety shack. "I can still see Childe standing by the cliff-edge, staring with vague intentness into immensity", recalled Lindsay (1958: 136). Childe's "amiably withering comments" and his rôle "as a bubble pricker, a mildly caustic iconoclast, whose glasses took on an unholy glitter as he demolished somebody's illusions with sardonic kindness" were other Lindsay memories of those halcyon days in the bush.

All this satisfaction must have confirmed the censor's worst fears, when he read Childe's cheery letter to Miles: "Your introductions were most handy", Childe told him,[18] "and have given me great assistance with the various ministers". "There is a refreshing air of revolutionary optimism up here", Childe continued, "There certainly is far more freedom and one does not find oneself faced with an army of plain clothes note-takers at the Trades Hall on Sunday nights". Yet Childe reckoned without the censor's vigilant note-taking; and Queensland politics soon lost their pristine charm for him, as *How Labour governs* later revealed.

Late in 1918, Childe suddenly found a classics mastership thrust upon him by eager political comrades. In November he commenced teaching at Maryborough Grammar School, over 100 miles north of Brisbane. Raymond Evans (in press) has reconstructed the extraordinary sequence of events by which the governing board of this conservative private school was replaced by trustees nominated by the Queensland Labor government. When teachers resigned, leaving pupils without masters shortly before the annual examinations, Childe was offered a post to commence immediately. Without any prior reference to the disaffected headmaster, Childe was escorted to the school by the local Labor Member of Parliament, and deposited unceremoniously as the relieving classics master.

This was scarcely the way to pedagogic success or job satisfaction, and the boys ensured that his class proved difficult to manage; the headmaster's antagonism was even made public when he wrote to the local newspaper:[19] "On Tuesday, 29th October, at 9.00 am" the headmaster reported, "Mr Child

[sic] arrived at the school personally conducted by Mr Weir, MLA. Mr Weir handed him over to me, to be numbered among the staff, but without volunteering any statement in regard to him".

Although the war was nearing its end, Childe's presence coincided with a "march for freedom" and a recruiting drive, in which school cadets (his class) participated. It is relevant to public reaction, however, that of the 180 old boys who had enlisted, 40 had been killed. Accompanying these martial activities came 64 marchers who had to be billeted (presumably including some in Childe's hotel). So did Sergeant William Brown, an undercover intelligence officer. It is no surprise, therefore, that the parent with whom Brown was billeted complained in a letter to the *Maryborough Chronicle*[20]that the new classics master was "a member of the peace alliance . . . I have two sons at the school, and wish their education to be continued on British lines . . .

At a meeting in the Town Hall upon the following evening there was plain speaking. The Reverend L. Toshach spoke of "the man who talks peace". Such persons, he affirmed (while quoting the gospels) "were no good to this country, and they should be sent to Germany". Sergeant Brown was equally forthright, when inciting recruitment:[21]

> . . . a message had been given by the people of Australia in 1914, promising the boys at the front the last man and the last shilling, but the country had not fulfilled that promise . . . [interjection] . . . Sergeant Brown: "Keep your mouth shut or you will fall in". In your own town, proceeded the speaker, you have a pacifist, and there is no need to mention his name. Such men as these believe in peace without indemnities and annexations.

Meanwhile, back in Brisbane, an irritable Laurence Childe wrote to his sister Alice,[22] "Have you heard of Gordon's appointment to Maryborough . . . and the question that was asked of the Minister for Education in the Legislative Assembly . . . As it was featured in the newspaper, you can imagine the publicity given to the appointment . . . his connection with us must be apparent to all". He continued, "I can well imagine the effect it will have on the parents of the boys up there. It's hardly likely they'd let their boys come under the influence (if Gordon has any influence) of one with such a record as G's. A man who would apparently sacrifice his country, and from his utterances seems to sympathize with our enemies".

As a class member later recalled (Evans, in press), Childe was subjected to unmerciful treatment by the class. Being a pacifist, "Childe was for it . . . Commencing with a low verbal barrage, the attack developed as the weeks went by and converted to physical form when all class members equipped themselves with pea-shooters. These would be operated either as individual sniping weapons or in co-ordinated group fire from different angles, or as a concentrated all-class volley".

Public humiliation continued in the newspaper, under the theme "Who is

Mr Child?"[sic]. The school's headmaster contributed a vitriolic response on the politics of Childe's appointment.[23] Mr Childe then answered the question himself with forceful dignity, spelling his name correctly and listing his academic credentials.[24] Having now assisted the "unfortunate" pupils to their examinations, Childe concluded:

> I do not feel it is the business of a scholar to struggle against the violence of reaction learnt at home . . . If, in future, the political opinions of masters, instead of their academic qualifications, are to be made the subject of inquisitorial researches . . . the future of education here will indeed be dark. If, moreover, when the persons in question are found to fail in the standards of political orthodoxy set up by this unseen tribunal, the methods of secret incitement to unruly pupils be continued, Maryborough may yet boast so unique an institution as a school for anarchists.

Ironically, one of the school cadets and a leading tormentor in Childe's class was Percy Reginald Stephensen. By 1921 he had joined the Communist Party; he later combined with Jack Lindsay in London in managing the Franfrolico Press, but returning to Australia during the 1930s he adopted neo-Fascism, a cause in which he was funded by W. J. Miles (Munro 1984).

The Maryborough scholastic year ended with speech night, addressed by the State Treasurer, E. G. Theodore, but boycotted by all the boys of the school. Childe then hastened back to Brisbane. "Childe's sensitive nature was not proof against the antagonism displayed by the scholars" sneered the vengeful censor.[25] Presumably this unhappy episode sufficed to end Childe's school-mastering ambitions. Early in January 1919, he was offered the position of classics master at Newington College, Stanmore, Sydney, but evidently he preferred employment as a clerk in the Queensland public service,[26] He must have agreed with Bert Evatt,[27] however, who commiserated that his work must be "very bloody dull and mechanical".

To what extent may these scarifying experiences have affected Childe's future life habits and bearing? Years later he told his friend R. Palme Dutt "that he would have chosen revolutionary politics but he found the price too high" (Green 1981: 57). This episode surely contributed towards raising that price. Jack Lindsay (1958: 135–6), his friend during these traumatic times, found that Childe "was not a person who unbosomed himself about his private affairs". While he was the "most detached person I knew", Lindsay "was never quite sure if he guarded his detachment as a defence against the bruises which a brutish world could so easily inflict on his too-tender sensibilities . . . His odd though likeable face, I felt certain, contributed to his refusal to come too far out of his inner refuge".

Fortunately for Childe's peace of mind, he soon obtained a temporary tutorship in the WEA, teaching economic thought, including Karl Marx. His activities during the following months have been examined closely by Raymond Evans (in press). While Witherby was out of Queensland during

March 1919, Childe briefly joined forces with some more radical socialists in an attempt to change the nature of the WEA. They sought its independence from university control, with direct working-class input. Childe backed down when Witherby returned and energetically fought the proposal.

One of Childe's speeches in this debate was summarized in the Brisbane Labor Party newspaper.[28] It is interesting, because Childe continued to express optimism and gratitude for the unique achievements and high standards of the Queensland government. Were these sentiments genuine, in view of his wrath expressed in *How Labour governs*? By then, he surely had observed the gulf separating reality from ideal, and there is little doubt that he had been the beneficiary of something akin to cronyism. Perhaps he felt that the price of local criticism was too high for the whole truth. His extravagant and personal-ized opinion of other Australian universities merits quotation, because his own experience was limited to Sydney.

Those institutions "produced snobs, scabs, and censors, as was the case in New South Wales, where a loyalty battalion had taken the place of strikers. In other states, though not in Queensland, university professors seemed to be chosen for their political beliefs and not for their intellectual attainment"

However, the University of Queensland soon joined their ranks. Childe applied for a temporary lectureship in classics during August 1919. When a local man with a single degree was appointed, the headlines in Labor's *Daily Standard* proclaimed "University Bias", "Brilliant Scholar Turned Down". The angry journalist who sketched Childe's academic qualifications, however, found Oxford's esoteric terminology confusing.[29] He credited Childe with "A First in Greets" unlike the *Maryborough Chronicle* which awarded him a First in "Grates"!

Finale

At this critical juncture Childe returned to Sydney, where he was appointed personal secretary to John Storey, the Labor Party Leader of the NSW Opposition and a political moderate. The appointment probably resulted from the intervention of William McKell, whom Childe had coached when McKell was preparing for a general qualifying examination for entrance to legal training. McKell acknowledged his debt to Childe years later (Kelly 1971: 21–2, 36). Evatt (1945: 489) remarked that Storey's success in attacking the government, "and the concentrated pungency of Storey's daily comments on the Government strongly suggested the brain of the classical scholar". It was following Storey's electoral victory in 1920 that Childe was sent to the NSW Agent-General's London office, thereby ending his Australian career. Stuart Piggott (1958: 311) envisaged Childe at that time "as a shy, idealistic, awkward young man". To those psychological ingredients must be added a strength of character willing to abide prejudice, misrepresentation, and a determination to achieve. Possibly, also, his self-reliance was strengthened, together with a distrust of the cronyism and networking in which he had been involved, but which he was to attack scathingly in *How Labour governs.*

In retrospect, the calibre or subsequent achievements of Gordon Childe's political and intellectual contacts are remarkable. He established close personal relationships with some of Australia's ablest Labor politicians. Evatt became leader of the Federal Labor party and played a significant rôle in establishing the United Nations. Storey, J. T. Lang and McKell were Premiers of New South Wales, while McKell later became Australian Governor-General. In Queensland, both T. J. Ryan and E. G. Theodore were premiers, while the latter and F. M. Forde both achieved the Deputy Prime Ministership of the Commonwealth.

Apart from the politicians, however, the *Australian Dictionary of Biography* includes as worthy of note most of those independent thinkers with whom Childe had contact. This selective survey includes entries on W. J. Miles, Bertha McNamara, M. J. O'Reilly, R. S. Ross and F. Sinclaire. In addition, many of Childe's contemporary participants in the WEA movement made contributions judged sufficiently significant for inclusion.

One scholar who was closely associated with the WEA, and also with Childe, was University of Queensland Professor of Philosophy, Elton Mayo. He departed in 1922 to achieve fame in America as a social theorist and industrial psychologist. The 1990 Brisbane Childe Conference was told by Gregory Melleuish (in press) that with the presence of Childe and Mayo "this was Brisbane's world historical moment" in the intellectual life of humanity when it was home of the two most significant innovative Australian social theorists"of this century.

During those lack-lustre inter-war years of generally conservative, conventional thought, Australia could ill spare Childe's vigorous intellect and logical focus. Whatever views are held concerning Childe's pacifist and political opinions, and no matter how one admires his resolve, or sympathizes with him over the indignities and academic rejection to which he was subjected, both personally and through the anonymity of the censor's venom-tipped pen, his actions must be assessed within the confines and ethos of Australian society three quarters of a century ago.

The following measured thoughts by one of Childe's Oxford professors, Francis J. Haverfield, written while Childe was resident in Brisbane, remain apposite advice, not only to Childe but to assessors of his Australian career:[30]

Your letter of 14th Sept has just arrived. I am distressed that things should have thus gone amiss with your university career in Sydney. I don't however know quite what I can do. At this distance it is impossible to form a clear idea of the circumstances. Generally, I have a great dislike to mixing up politics with learning. At the same time, I am bound to remember that learned men do sometimes say things which upset the politicians; and that, in university matters, action is occasionally taken on one ground and defended and justified on another – that is, that the reason for your trouble may not literally be that which you mention. People think the real reason is hard and unkind to mention: so they substitute another . . . Besides this, I do not know of any of the Sydney authorities and cannot well make any protest . . . I fear it will remain true that unpopular views *are* unpopular, and no indignation will get round this awkward fact. I am afraid that we in Europe will have a good deal of friction over the leavings of the war . . . I hope however that as feeling cools down gradually, you will find a career open to you without trouble. For a historian, it is a stirring time: every morning one wakes to find a monarch or monarchy gone: Europe's but a battered caravanserai.

Acknowledgements

The stimulation that came from participating in the 1990 Brisbane Conference on Gordon Childe proved crucial to my preparation of this paper. It was one of the most congenial and constructive conferences of my career, evidently a view shared by another participant (Beilharz 1991).

I am indebted, in particular, to Terry Irving, Department of Government, University of Sydney, and Raymond Evans, Department of History, University of Queensland, whose research provided the basis for my study. Dr Ian Jack, Senior Fellow, St Andrew's College, University of Sydney, assisted with information concerning Childe's residence in his college. Dr J. Stokes, Director of Access, Australian Archives, Canberra, and Mr F. T. Bryant, Australian Archives, Melbourne, facilitated my access to papers which, otherwise, would not have been available in time. Their co-operation is acknowledged with gratitude, as is the advice of Michael Richards, National Library of Australia. The paper was typed by Caren Florance.

Notes

1. Australian Archives Victoria MP95/1-167/57/68/ (QF2804), H. V. Evatt to V. G. Childe 3 Dec 1918
2. *NSW Parliamentary Debates* 71(1918): 394, 27 June
3. AA V MP95/1-1 68/8/1 4 Childe to O'Reilly, 12 June 1918
4. M V MP95/1-169/1/8 (MF904) Childe to F. J. Williams, 3 May 1918
5. AA V MP95/1-169/9/16 (MF1036) Childe to F. J. Williams, 22 May 1918
6. AA V MP95/1-168/15/20 (RE1207) Childe to Mrs McNamara, 16 Aug 1918
7. AA V MP95/1-169/35/42 (MF1628) Childe to F. Sinclaire, 20 Aug 1918
8. AA V MP95/1-168/15/20 (RE1070) J. R. McGrath to Childe, 15 July 1918
9. NSWPD72(1918): 1208 (McKell) 11 Sept; 1452-3 (Smith) 17 Sept
10. AA V MP95/1-168/21/29 (RE1241) Childe to O'Reilly, 27 Aug 1918

1a David Harris opening the Conference on 8 May 1992 by crowning the bust of Childe with a Central Asian hat similar to the one Childe wore for his final lectures at the Institute in 1956 (photograph by Stuart Laidlaw).

1b Conference speakers, chairmen, and former colleagues and students of Childe on the steps of the Institute, Gordon Square, London, 8 May 1992 (photograph by Stuart Laidlaw). From left to right, *front row*: Geraldine Talbot, Michael Rowlands, John Mulvaney, Kent Flannery, David Harris, Bruce Trigger, Leo Klejn; *back rows*: Katsuyuki Okamura, John Wilkes, Ellen Macnamara, Roy Hodson, Grahame Clark, Jay Butler, Sinclair Hood, Rachel Maxwell-Hyslop, Paul Mellars, Patricia Christie, Peter Gathercole, Charles Higham, George Eogan, Eve Evans, John Evans, Colin Renfrew.

2a Childe at Skara Brae, Orkney, 1929. The woman third from the right may be Margaret Cole (wife of G. D. H. Cole and sister of Raymond Postgate). Postgate visited Skara Brae in August 1929 with George Lansbury MP, who was First Commissioner of Works in Ramsay MacDonald's Labour Government. This photograph may have been taken on that occasion.

2b Childe at the entrance to the Museu de Sanfins, northern Portugal, December 1949; from left to right: unknown, Childe, Colonel Mário Cardozo (archaeologist), Miss Marion Jennings, Mrs Ruth Jennings (wife of the British Consul in Oporto).

3a Childe (wearing his famous "drainers" and black felt hat), Grahame Clark and others on a Prehistoric Society visit to Dartmoor, September 1949.

3b Childe "in the field" during a Prehistoric Society Study Tour to Cumbria, September 1948.

3c Childe at the site of Ruse, Bulgaria, April 1955.

3d Childe at Kazanluk, Bulgaria, April 1995.

4a Childe in his room at the Institute of Archaeology, St John's Lodge, Regent's Park, London (probably 1955 or 1956).

4b The Institute's staff outside St John's Lodge in 1955. From left to right, *front row*: Maurice Cookson, Kathleen Kenyon, Sheppard Frere, Max Mallowan, Gordon Childe, Frederick Zeuner, Edward Pyddoke, Joan du Plat Taylor, Ione Gedye; *middle row*: Marjorie Conlon, Rachel Maxwell-Hyslop, Arthur ApSimon, Ian Cornwall, Geraldine Talbot, Olive Starkey; *back row*: Mr and Mrs Dance, Mary Pinsett, Jennifer Banham, Penny Brooks, Joan Sheldon, Judy Phillips, Marjorie Maitland Howard, Harry Stewart.

11. AA V MP95/1-169/35/42 (MF1628) Childe to Sinclaire, 20 Aug 1918 and attachment
12. AA V MP95/1-167/36/45 (QF1827) W. J. Miles to E. M. Free MLA, 10 Sept 1918
13. AA V MP95/1-168/21/29 R S Ross to W. J Miles, 18 Sept 1918
14. AA V MP95/1-167/36/145 (QF1829) P. Brookfield to C. Butler, 10 Sept 1918
15. M V MP95/1-168/8/14 (RE1034) Alice [Childe] to V. G. Childe, 8 July 1918
16. AA V MP95/1-167/56 (QF2278) A. S. Kennedy to Childe, 14 Oct 1918
17. M V MP95/1-168/21/29 (ER1391) Childe to W. J Miles, 17 Oct 1918
18. ibid
19. *Maryborough Chronicle* 21 Nov 1918, p6 col 5
20. ibid. 31 Oct 1918 p4 col 3-4; 1 Nov 1918 p6 col 4
21. ibid. 4 Nov 1918 p6 col 4-5
22. AA V MP95/1-67/46/56 (QF2337) L Childe to Sister Vernon [Childe], 10 Nov 1918
23. *Maryborough Chronicle* 21 Nov 1918 p6 col 5
24. ibid. 29 Nov 1918
25. Speech night: *Maryborough Chronicle* 5 Dec 1918 p6; M V MP95/1-167/69/76 (QF2849) C. Pescott to Childe 7 Jan 1919
26. ibid.
27. AA V MP95/1-167/69/76 (QF2546) Evatt to Childe, 6 Jan 1919
28. *Daily Standard* (Brisbane) 26 Mar 1919
29. ibid; *Maryborough Chronicle* 1 Nov 1918 p6 col 4
30. AA V MP95/1-167/69/76 (QF2776) F. Haverfield to Childe, 3 Nov 1918.

References

Allen, J. 1981. Perspectives of a sentimental journey. V. Gordon Childe in Australia 1917–1921. *Australian Archaeology* 12, 1–12.

Beilharz, P. 1991. The Vere Gordon Childe Centenary Conference. *Labour History* 60, 108–12.

Cain, F. 1983. *The origins of political surveillance in Australia.* Sydney: Angus & Robertson.

Childe, V. G. 1923. *How Labour governs.* London: Labour Publishing Company.

Childe, V. G. 1947. *History.* London: Cobbett Press.

Evans, R., in press. Vere Gordon Childe in Queensland 1918–19. In *Childe and Australia: archaeology, politics and ideas*, T. Irving, G. Melleuish, P. Gathercole (eds). Brisbane: University of Queensland Press.

Evatt, H. V. 1945. *Australian Labor leader.* Sydney: Angus & Robertson.

Fitzhardinge, L. F. 1990. W. J. Woodhouse. *Australian Dictionary of Biography*, vol. 12, 561–2. Melbourne: Melbourne University Press.

Green, S. 1981. *Prehistorian: a biography of V. Gordon Childe.* Bradford-on-Avon, England: Moonraker Press.

Kelly, V. 1971. *A man of the people.* Sydney: Alpha Books.

Lindsay, J. 1958. *Life rarely tells.* London: Bodley Head.

Melleuish, G., in press. The place of V. Gordon Childe in Australian intellectual history. In *Childe and Australia: archaeology, politics and ideas*, T. Irving, G. Melleuish, P. Gathercole (eds). Brisbane: University of Queensland Press.

Mulvaney, D. J. 1949. Some influences on the early Australian Labor Party. *Twentieth Century* (Melbourne) 3, 34–49.

Mulvaney, D. J. 1990. From *The dawn* to sunset: Gordon Childe in Melbourne, 1957.

Australian Archaeology **30**, 29–31.
Munro, C. 1984. *Wild man of letters. The story of P. R. Stephensen.* Melbourne: Melbourne University Press.
O'Neil, W. M. 1979. Sir Francis Anderson. *Australian Dictionary of Biography*, vol. 7, 53–5. Melbourne: Melbourne University Press.
Piggott, S. 1958. Vere Gordon Childe. *Proceedings of the British Academy* **44**, 305–12.
Ravetz, A. 1959. On Gordon Childe. *The New Reasoner* **10**, 56–66.
St Andrew's 1918. *The St Andrew's Magazine* **16**(November), 12.
Walker, D. R. 1988. Frederick Sinclaire. *Australian Dictionary of Biography*, vol. 11, 615–16. Melbourne: Melbourne University Press.

Discussion
CHAIRED BY ROY HODSON

Gathercole: I also was at the Brisbane meeting, and perhaps it would be appropriate, since this is the session dealing with Childe in Australia, to amplify some of the points made by John and to take up one or two other related questions. The really interesting thing in Australian political studies and history, is (and I agree with John here) that the period of the First World War is undergoing a great deal of study at present, and the research is very impressive indeed. John referred to Terry Irving's work and I think his analysis is pre-eminent, particularly his re-examination of *How Labour governs.* I want to say this now because I, like other people, have misunderstood that book and have, worse, actually misunderstood it in print. It is not, according to Irving, ultimately a negative work. I can't summarize his arguments in any detail, but his paper in the Australian journal *Politics*, in 1988, stresses the point that Childe actually believed in the future of the Labor Party in Australia. It was the policies of the Labor Party that he was lambasting so vehemently. In other words, it was not a classic Marxist attack on English-speaking social democracy.

One of John's points, which I would like to emphasize, is that Australian Labor politics at this time were extremely volatile. There people spoke out very strongly in contradistinction to what was the rule in this country. And Australian Labor politics were not an Antipodean replication of what was being said here. I think it is very important to realize that Childe did see a future for the Labor Party in Australia, for what we might call Australian social democracy. In that sense, he did not leave Australia, in my view, disillusioned. Indeed, I think the disillusionment about the future was there much earlier in his consciousness. There is a gloomy letter to Gilbert Murray (written in the spring of 1917 shortly before he took Greats) in which he asks Murray, who has just returned to England from Australia (I paraphrase): "Can I come and get some advice from you? There is no future for me here, no future for me in Australia, I suspect because of my heretical opinions. Should I emigrate to the United States?" And Murray, who was of course Australian by birth, annotated it: "Curious. A very clever archaeologist; Australian. I have asked him to lunch on Sunday and walk".

Another point I want to make concerns the question of whether there is continuity in Childe's thinking from this extraordinary period in Australia, which ended with his being sacked in London by a new incoming government in New South Wales of a different hue, and his subsequent thinking. It is interesting to note that the first review of *How Labour governs* was by Raymond Postgate in 1923 in *The Plebs*, which was the journal of the National Council of Labour Colleges. It is a very good criticism of the book and its limitations. Of course Childe knew Postgate at Oxford, and, incidentally, Postgate visited Skara Brae with George Lansbury in August 1929 (Fig. 3). It is interesting to note that Childe himself started to review for *The Plebs* in 1924, and did so on and off right through until 1944. There were 16 reviews and two articles in all. Now, these publications were expressions of his links with the Left throughout this period and the reviews were generally in politics and anthropology rather than archaeology. The first review was of Pember Reeves' book, *State experiments in Australia and New Zealand*, which had just been re-issued, a study in Fabianism of course. The next was of a book by J. K. Heydon on wage-slavery, and the third was a review of two books by Perry, *The origin of magic and religion* and *The growth of civilization*. All three appeared in *The Plebs* in 1924. Now these are only small indications of the degree, as it were, of the continuity from Australia to England of Childe's political and intellectual activities on the Left.

Mulvaney: As Peter has mentioned the Brisbane conference, I would like to say that it was the most exciting conference I have been to and I really recommend everyone to buy the proceedings, which are being edited by Irving, Melleuish and Gathercole, and are due to be published this year. It was full of fascinating views, not only about Childe himself but about the general influences with which he grew up.

Hill: What we have heard is very interesting because in my experience the atmosphere which Childe encountered – conflict with the security people and so on – persisted in Australia for quite a long time. After the war in the 1950s, for instance, there was a case almost exactly analogous with that of Childe, when a literary adviser of my firm (which was established in Australia at that time), who was a most eminent historian with a worldwide reputation, was denied a job in the University of Sydney on the basis of a secret police report, not into his current political activities but into his pre-war, student days. This caused such an outcry that one of the leading academics of the University of Sydney resigned and came and set up in Oxford. This is probably well known to some of you. There seems somehow to have been an extreme, almost caricature-like relationship between certain public bodies and academics in Australia.

Mulvaney: As an Australian, I can defend it in one sense, but what I meant to say before was that the censorship in Australia, which began in 1917 continued until the total armistice was signed late in 1919. They continued censoring the mail for a year after the war ended, and certainly censorship in the 1950s was not unlike the McCarthy era in America, but it did rather depend upon one's university: some universities were far less liberal than others.

Harris: I would like to ask, as we have John and Peter here together, if there is any evidence that Childe ever paid any attention to the pre-European history of Australia, either during his early sojourn there or subsequently?

Mulvaney: Well, I will answer first, being the speaker. I had him in my office at the University of Melbourne – I was doing my first excavation in Australia and had spread out all the stone tools. He spent two minutes looking at them, and then wished me luck – he had no interest in them whatsoever. I spent a day driving him up to the hills to look for lyre birds and we did not talk about Australian archaeology at any time, as far as I can remember. There is also a letter which he wrote to Mrs Mary Alice Evatt in which he said that there were scarcely any archaeologists being trained in Australia. I subsequently found out that the letter was written before he met me! I have said in print that he also showed little interest in Australian Aboriginal anthropology and, although he made some references to it, they are extremely rare. Given the amount of use that, say, Sir James Frazer made of Australian evidence – and he would have been familiar with that – it is a little surprising.

Gathercole: There is a letter to Crawford, written in August 1957, where he mentions the possibilities of Australian archaeology. And, strangely enough, I wrote to him at the Institute here in September 1957 asking for a reference for a job in New Zealand and he, to my amazement, not only wrote back from Australia but sent me the reference to send on, because he said he was moving around an awful lot. I have got the very letter here, and I will just quote one little bit from it: "There is urgent need out here for someone with up-to-date techniques and notions to make a serious study of S. Pacific technology. There is much material here, some of it rapidly deteriorating, but Mulvaney is the only man with first-class techniques to tackle it seriously". The real tragedy of this, from my point of view, was that the letter was dated 7 October and he died on 19 October. I could not even reply to it, but obviously he sent me the reference because he was going to commit suicide and I had the extraordinary experience of typing it up, from his handwritten script, and sending it to Otago. But the point that I am making is that, in the reference and in his note and in the letter to Crawford, he does recognize that there are archaeological possibilities not just in Australia but in the South Pacific, and he was anxious for me to go, not so much because it was me, but because it was somebody who could go out there, as it were, and join John.

Rowlands: I was wondering if there is a link between the censorship of academics in Australia before the war and the sending of troops to fight in the defence of Western civilization in Europe, and Childe's pacifism and his own intellectual interest in Indo-European origins. Does this help to explain his lack of interest in Australian pre-colonial Aboriginal archaeology?

Mulvaney: Well, as I indicated, Australians certainly had a deep dedication to the First World War and were very bellicose. Childe was certainly not alone in being an opponent of the war; in fact there was quite a big pacifist movement in Australia. But that is not really answering your question, and I don't know that I can.

Maxwell-Hyslop: I think it might be recorded that when McCarthysim was rife in America – we were discussing it at the early Institute – the staff all came to the conclusion that if there was any backlash on the Director, we would all go to jail with him.

Glover: This is an anecdote really, but something just triggered off a memory. When I first came to the Institute, John Waechter, who was then teaching Palaeolithic Archaeology, said "You come from Australia" and handed me a central Australian spear saying, "Childe usually had that. He used to use this in his lectures and it is broken because he threw it at someone to demonstrate spear-throwing". I believe that it is the very one he is holding in the sketch of him by Marjorie Maitland Howard that David Harris showed at the start of the conference (Frontispiece). It is still in my room and I shall present it to him for the Institute archives. Maybe, there we have a symbol of Childe's latent interest in Australian prehistory!

References

Heydon, J. K. 1924. *Wage-slavery*. London: Bodley Head.

Irving, T. 1988. New light on *How Labour governs*: re-discovered political writings by V. Gordon Childe. *Politics* **23**(1), 70–7.

Irving, T., G. Melleuish, P. Gathercole (eds), in press. *Childe and Australia: archaeology, politics and ideas*. Brisbane: University of Queensland Press.

Perry, W. J. 1923. *The origin of magic and religion*. London: Methuen.

Perry, W. J. 1924. *The growth of civilization*. London: Methuen.

Reeves, W. P. 1923. *State experiments in Australia and New Zealand* [2 vols]. London: Allen & Unwin.

Childe and Soviet archaeology
A romance

LEO S. KLEJN

The life of Childe resembles a knight's romance. His lady-love was Soviet archaeology (the word "archaeology" is feminine in Russian). The Knight was bold, unselfish, full of noble deeds and very lonely. The Dame was young, fresh and innovative, but, as is clear today, capricious, calculating, lying and liable to overestimate her merits. With such a combination the romance, although mutual, could not end happily.

It is known that the Knight did not become enamoured at once – he forced himself to love this distant foreigner out of a feeling of duty. This was love by conviction. The signs of her attention pleased him, but in secret he suffered deeply from her wicked temper and tormented himself with doubts. Finally he became sadly disillusioned and it was that disillusion which contributed to his suicide. As Daniel (1958: 66) said, "Childe's attitude to Soviet archaeological scholarship changed during his lifetime".

It is less known in the West that the Dame also did not fall in love with the Knight at first sight. Neither did she love him wholeheartedly, nor for those merits which united them in the eyes of strangers. Their last meeting occurred when the Knight had already become disillusioned with his sweetheart; however, shy by nature, he said no harsh words, but on his return he sent her a letter that she must have considered insulting, and put an end to his life. The Dame, although perplexed by the message of his strange death, read this letter in silence and then kept it a deep secret – until now.

All that I have described here metaphorically has its exact correspondence in reality.

The first acquaintance

The first reaction of Soviet archaeologists to Childe's work was evidently negative. *The dawn of European civilization* was frankly diffusionist, *The Aryans* was even worse, migrationist; indeed, Childe himself considered it too near to Kossinna's constructions (Trigger 1980: 173–4). Diffusionism and migrationism were phenomena to which Soviet archaeologists of the 1920s were deeply antagonistic.

In 1931 a biting review by Bogaevskij of the short article by Childe (1930) on the relations of the Aegean and the Balkans appeared in the *Soobščenija* ("Messages") of GAIMK. The review, entitled "On the question of migrations theory" (Bogaevskij 1931), clearly placed Childe in the enemy camp. Childe's article, wrote Bogaevskij (1931: 35) "depicts very well the typical position of the bourgeois scholars who maintain the migrationist point of view . . . " Bogaevskij declared unconvincing Childe's constructions on the hiatus between Palaeolithic and Mesolithic in southern Europe and on the migration of agriculturalists from the southeastern Mediterranean: these constructions were built purely formally, on the comparison of ceramics. Bogaevskij (1931: 37) undertook an "analysis of the methodological means of research work of Childe as a representative of West-European bourgeois scholarship which may be correctly understood only by using Lenin's thesis on the partisanship of knowledge".

Having accused Childe of "formalism" and "narrow empiricism", Bogaevskij ended his review with an inimitable passage:

> From a materialist point of view . . . Childe's Anatolians driven by an irrepressible desire to move with their pottery up the Danube after having exhausted the soil of Asia Minor . . . are like the jobless workers of England, who signal the decay of British capitalism, tell-tale evidence which testifies to the stagnating state of . . . West-European scholarship and to the unlimited possibilities of fruitful scholarly research in the USSR. (Bogaevskij 1931: 38)

The dangerous Marxist

From the early 1930s, after Childe had written his main diffusionist works, there begins a period in his life which Grahame Clark (1976: 4) described as the time "after Childe", because for him all was finished for Childe at that point. However, Childe himself regarded this period as the time of his proper maturity, as distinct from the earlier period in which some of his ideas were in his opinion "childish, not Childeish" (Childe 1958b: 70). This new period was the time of his intensive rethinking of prehistory in the spirit of Marxism, which led, by the mid-1930s, to his conceptions of the Neolithic and Urban Revolutions in *New light on the most ancient East* (1934).

It was then, in 1935, that Childe went for the first time to the Soviet Union, and familiarized himself with "some typical Russian works on prehistory"; "From Kruglov and Podgayetsky, Krichevskiĭ and Tretyakov" he wrote at the end of his life "I learned how neatly even the Marrist perversion of Marxism explained without appeal to undocumented external factors the development of certain prehistoric cultures in the Union" (Childe 1958b: 71–2).

Between 1940 and 1946 he published in *Man* and in *Nature* several surveys of Soviet archaeological literature (Childe 1940, 1942, 1943, 1944, 1945a,

1946a). In these articles he showed that, having mastered Russian, he was now seriously analyzing Russian literature, but he saw only the outer side of the Soviet reality. For example, he did not know that the real author of the book *The clan society of the steppes of eastern Europe*, which so enraptured him, was Latynin and not Kruglov and Podgayetskij, whose names appeared as the authors. Latynin had been arrested not long before Childe's arrival and disappeared from the archaeological milieu for two decades; Kruglov and Podgayetskij were Latynin's young helpers and they put their names on his work in order to save it. But when Latynin returned (as an incredibly emaciated invalid) at the time of the so-called Late Rehabilitance (sic) they both were already dead: one fell on the battlefield, the other died from hunger in the siege of Leningrad, and Latynin could not bring himself to delete their names from his book.[1] Kričevskij was a clever man known for his ability to cite not merely quotations from the classics of Marxism by heart but also the appropriate volume and page numbers. But he was known also as a person seriously suspected of secretly denouncing his colleagues (he too died in the siege of Leningrad). In 1946 in his well known book *Scotland before the Scots*, the most provocative of all his Marxist books, Childe wrote concerning local prehistory: "I decided to adapt to it the method so brilliantly applied by E. Yu. Krichevskii, A. P. Kruglov, G. V. Podgayetskii, P. N. Tretyakov and other Marxists to Russian prehistory" (Childe 1946b: v); and he expressed his gratitude to Russian colleagues "whose mastership inspired him" (Childe 1946b: vii).

What was the attitude towards Childe in the USSR during this period of the 1930s and early 1940s? As it was in general towards Western leftists: favourable, but watchful. He was allowed to come to the USSR, and they scrutinized attentively how he referred thereafter to Soviet affairs. They were satisfied with his behaviour, but did not applaud him, did not refer positively to him, and did not translate his publications. Books by Osborn and Crawford were translated, but Childe's were not. As a scholar he scarcely existed for the world of Soviet archaeology.

This apparent anomaly can be explained. The point is that for the bolshevik ideologists the most dangerous enemies were thought to be not the frankly right-wing figures, conservatives and reactionaries, but the non-bolshevik politicians from the left wing, their nearest neighbours according to political positions and their competitors in the struggle for proletarian souls. In the USSR there was no worse label than "Trotskyist". As in the clerical milieu; you can find a common language with hierarchs of other religions, but you must burn your own dissidents and sectarians. A Marxist of non-bolshevik persuasion can only be a revisionist, provocateur or renegade. Thus, the fact that Childe was a Marxist, but not a strictly dependable or governable one, did not draw him closer to Soviet archaeology, did not make him quite "ours", but turned him into an alien and dangerous figure, as if he were contagious, though nevertheless useful.

The period of Childe's intensively Marxist interpretations was reflected in Soviet archaeological literature after some delay. In 1947 *Vestnik Leningradskogo Universiteta* ("Herald of Leningrad University") published an expansive and very sympathetic review of Childe's *Scotland before the Scots* by Artamonov, who was one of the initiators of Soviet archaeology and had been Director of the Institute of Archaeology in the Academy of Sciences of the USSR. Artamonov, who was later to become Director of the Hermitage Museum and Pro-Rector of Leningrad University, was a clever and broad-minded person. He appreciated that it was necessary to introduce Childe into Soviet literature and to give his work a positive reception, but he also realized that if Childe were introduced as a Marxist he would be ignored, so he refrained from mentioning Childe's Marxist convictions in his review.

"In the works of this scholar", Artamonov wrote (1947: 111), "a remarkable evolution may be perceived, in which the book under review takes quite an exclusive position, signifying a new stage in the world outlook of the scholar. Gordon Childe's former works, distinguished by their advanced spirit and wide scholarly horizons, enormous erudition and excellent facility for generalizations, remained methodologically attached to the positions usual for bourgeois historical scholarship. Race is a creative agent in them, and changes in cultural phenomena are attributed to influences and endless migrations. Independent development concerned the author very little". This was untrue, and Artamonov was also wrong in that *Scotland before the Scots* did not start a new stage but terminated the previous one; the new stage really started at the beginning of the 1950s.

Artamonov also states (1947: 111) that Childe became aware of the rôle of independent development as a result of his acquaintance with the works of Soviet archaeologists. He especially notes in Childe's book "the recognition of the priority of Marxist over bourgeois scholarly methodology and his affirmation of the successes of Soviet archaeology"; and he exclaims: "not every bourgeois scholar would be bold enough to acknowledge its fruitlessness". Is the hint clear? Childe is a bourgeois scholar who has recognized the priority of Marxist Soviet scholarship, not a Marxist who avoided following strictly orthodox Soviet prescriptions. For anybody who did not guess, the point is reiterated: "I need not dwell for long on the methodological blunders of the author who uses for the first time the sharp weapons of true scholarly research and who still has not mastered it with the proper skill" (p. 118). And even more clearly: "Archaeology completely uncovers the material base of historical development . . . and often pushes even research workers distant from Marxism to spontaneous materialism" (pp. 120–21). It is Childe who, distant from Marxism, is a spontaneous materialist. The "author's materialism" continues Artamonov, "is mechanistic, not dialectical; the relations between basis and substructures are much more complex than the author thinks" (p. 120).

Artamonov minutely and with evident delight exposes the brilliant ideas of

Childe, now and again tapping him on the shoulder and scolding him gently for "groundless speculations"; "the importance of the external factor in development is clearly hyperbolized"; "the stages of Childe are not stages at all, they are simply periods of concrete development"; "patriarchy is questionable, rather here was matriarchy"; and so on. "We are sure", the reviewer concludes, that "this book is not an episode in the scholarly evolution of the archaeologist, it is rather the first experience which will be followed by other, more mature and perfect works" (p. 120). However, Soviet archaeology was, alas, itself not sufficiently mature to receive "more mature" or even "less mature" works of Childe.

After this approving treatment in the press, translations of Childe's works were to be expected. The trial balloon was a little book from the intensively Marxist period of Childe's creation, but the most inexpressive in this respect: *Progress and archaeology* (Childe 1945b). It was translated in 1949 with a preface by Arcikhovskij, a professor at Moscow University and one of the founders of Soviet archaeology. He was the person who at this time determined the shape of its, so to speak, mainstream. Arcikhovskij praised Childe unprecedentedly and excessively for his progressive views and mainly for his friendly attitude to the Soviet Union. The political support of foreigners was always more important to those in power than the similarity or divergence of ideas, and in the circumstances of the beginning of the Cold War and the isolation of the Soviet Union this became particularly important.

"Among the outrageous archaeologists of the capitalist world", Arcikhovskij wrote of Childe, "he alone showed an awareness of wide cultural–historical problems, he alone uses his brilliant erudition for studying the progressive development of ancient cultures. On this basis arose his portentous interest to Soviet scholarship, propagandist of which he was bold enough to become . . . " (Arcikhovskij 1949: 5). "Only he recognized our scholarship as advanced, and advanced as judged by the method it applied. His statements against the reactionary trends dominant in bourgeois archaeological scholarship, against formal typology, migrationism . . . and racism became sharper and more far-reaching. He declared in print that the exhibition at the Edinburgh Museum was reconstructed by him according to the model of the Moscow Historical Museum . . . "(pp. 6–7). And "Childe remains firm not only in his scholarly but also in his political sympathies. In November 1947 he was a speaker in the meeting devoted to the thirtieth anniversary of the Great October Socialist Revolution" (p. 8). Arcikhovskij also quotes from the preface to *Scotland before the Scots* where Childe refers to his dependence on Soviet scholars, and he defends Childe against his English colleagues: "In response to that, a review appeared in a leading English anthropological-ethnographical journal *Man*, in February 1947, by a certain Stuart Piggott who sharply attacked Childe for subordination to dangerous influences" (p. 8).

On Childe's book itself, *Progress and archaeology*, Arcikhovskij writes with restraint and he does so rather critically. Childe's world outlook seems to him "eclectic". "The main task of Soviet archaeology is the study of social-economical formations, and Childe in the book under review does not concern himself with this question". Childe speaks "on production and on techniques and scarcely considers social relations . . . There is no chapter on social relations although the author could have written one as there is rather a lot of archaeological material on this topic". Arcikhovskij rejected the conceptions of Neolithic and Urban Revolutions: why resort to euphemisms? The question is on the emergence of class relations and of class struggle – so let us speak directly! He was sceptical about the discovery of dwellings of the middle class – archaeology always finds palaces and huts. In brief, he detected "incorrect inferences" in the book, although he did say that it "will be useful for our reader who is armed with the learning of Marxism–Leninism" (p. 16). However, the reader armed with this learning took no notice of the book. And for some time the name of Childe in the USSR was honoured only for its propaganda value.

In 1951 Arcikhovskij's pupil Mongajt wrote in his article *The crisis of bourgeois archaeology*:

Among bourgeois scholars there are not only our ideological enemies. There are also progressive scholars there, friends of our country, who understand very well the worldwide significance of Soviet scholarship. Among such English scholars is Gordon Childe. Childe has not yet succeeded in overcoming many of the errors of bourgeois scholarship. But he understands that the scientific truth is in the Socialist camp and is not ashamed to call himself a pupil of Soviet archaeologists. (Mongajt 1951: 15)

Later Mongajt wrote to me, saying that he was ashamed of this article and begging me never to quote it. However, Daniel (1958: 66) remembered "vividly the delight with which he (Childe) would quote the passage from Mongajt's *The crisis in bourgeois archaeology*".

Tardy love

In 1945, ten years after his first visit, Childe visited Russia again. After returning he admired, in a letter to Braidwood, the signs of liberalization in Soviet life. Thus, a Soviet anthropologist had told Childe that, in his opinion, the bearers of Fatyanovo culture had invaded their territory (Trigger 1983: 4). Childe could not guess that this story did not in the least imply liberalization: at this time whole peoples were being deported and persecutions of the "cosmopolites" and the struggle for Russian "priorities" were starting. It was not a matter of liberalization; simply that the ideological line was changed. In accordance with the need to stimulate patriotic feelings and great-power ambitions, the problems of ethnogenesis came to the fore and they began to be solved by reference to migrations and even influences (although only in an admissible direction).

So began the postwar period, the late Stalin and early Khruščov years in the Soviet Union, the last period of Childe's life when he entered deeply into the methodological and philosophical problems of archaeology, and tried to bring archaeology into the realm of proper and relevant science. That he remained Marxist can be seen from his article (written in 1949 or 1950) *Prehistory and Marxism* (Childe 1979) and his *Social evolution* (1951). It was just at this time that Soviet archaeology discovered Childe for itself: he began to be read (at first in English), studied, then translated. But which Childe? Childe the diffusionist?; Childe of the 1920s, the former enemy!; Childe of the 1930s? Childe the Marxist remained dangerous; Childe of the 1950s, the thinker and scientist, was not yet interesting. It was only Childe of the 1920s (the same who was esteemed by Grahame Clark) who now appeared timely and to their liking.

It is no accident that just at the same time another figure entered Soviet archaeology, namely Kossinna, with his ethnic interpretation of cultures (*ethnische Deutung*), his retrospective method, and his assumption of migrations and continuity. Kossinna was not an outright migrationist: he defended autochthonous development in relation to his Germans and was a migrationist in explaining changes around them. Soviet archaeologists did the same, substituting Slavs or their forerunners for the Germans (Klejn 1974a: 9). As a matter of fact, Childe was accepted in the USSR side-by-side with Kossinna, as his twin. However, Kossinna entered Soviet scholarship in an underhand way and had to be severely criticized, whereas Childe was received legally.

In the late 1940s, when I was a student at Leningrad University, I studied fervently and, being short-sighted, sat in the first row in lectures which I held dear so that I could see what was on the lecturer's table just in front of me. Thus, I remember, when Professor Artamonov gave his course on Bronze Age archaeology, an English book appeared regularly on his table, open at the relevant page. It was Childe's *The dawn of European civilization*. Both we and our teacher were gripped by its clear construction, its all-embracing system, its unity. The entire mosaic of cultures and monuments were ordered in a way that made sense. The shock that Western archaeologists experienced in the late 1920s, we experienced in the late 1940s. But we, the enlightened, were still very few.

Then translations of Childe's major works began to appear. In 1952 *The dawn* was finally translated into Russian (from the fifth English edition of 1950) and published with a preface by Mongajt. This Soviet archaeologist continued the line of Artamonov and Arcikhovskij (his teacher), and conducted the same cunning game. Childe is never described as a Marxist, as he usually was in the West. A different title was allotted to him: "The Most Eminent Progressive Scholar".

Among archaeologists of Capitalist countries the most eminent progress-

ive scholar is Gordon Childe. Of course, Childe suffers from many
errors of bourgeois scholarship. But this is a scholar who seeks the truth
and who is sure that only the materialist understanding of the world
can help him in these searches. He understands that scientific truth is in
the camp of Socialism and he is not afraid to call himself a pupil of
Soviet archaeologists. (Mongajt 1952: 3–4)

Thus was Childe saved from excessive and dangerous pretensions. What
would be inexcusable for a Marxist was quite justifiable for a person originally
hostile to Marxism and now merely a progressive scholar, a diligent pupil of
Soviet archaeologists; one who had still not completed his education.

Perhaps Mongajt was cleverer than his ideological censors and one should
read him between the lines. Maybe, however, he was lead by intuition and
was not fully aware of his own rather heretical preferences. It was, obviously,
still impossible to write openly about why the book was so attractive for
Soviet archaeologists. Therefore, he wrote that the main validity of the book
was that it abounds in exact scrupulously documented facts, that the author
repudiates formal-typological method, rejects migrations and so on. The main
principle of the book, namely diffusionism, is considered in the preface to be
an erroneous idea. However, Mongajt scarcely adduces any objections to the
idea and offers almost nothing with which to refute it. The only suggestion
is that cultural borrowings are usually reformed in the area where they are
received. In contrast, the essence of diffusionism is depicted so clearly that it
becomes evident that it is the main topic in the book, and that because of this
the book is interesting.

In the concluding part of the preface, Mongajt writes: "Because Childe has
not understood the basic laws of historical development, he gives a motley
picture of various cultures, or cultural zones as he calls them . . . " (1952: 15).
How wide of the mark! Then on the honest hesitations of Childe: "Naturally,
absence of a monistic view of history leads the author to subjectivism" (pp.
15–16). This is to suppose that Mongajt at that time, with his monistic view,
could have written a similar book without any subjectivism. In fact, he really
did write such a book (Mongajt 1973–6), but at a later time, and there he
recognized still more clearly the hypothetical nature of the results. Nevertheless, in the sixth edition of *The dawn* (1957) Childe reworked the book and,
according to his words, weakened its "dogmatic orientalism" as a result of
Mongajt's critique in the preface to the Russian edition.

In 1954, a translation of another of Childe's major books was published:
New light on the most ancient East (1934) based on the fourth English edition
which had appeared in 1952. The original publication of this book, in 1934,
marked a turning point in Childe's rethinking of Marxist prehistory. It was
in it that his concepts of the Neolithic and Urban Revolutions were first fully
elaborated. However, the evidence presented in it served to broaden the basis
of diffusionism. One should not forget that Childe wrote in the book:
"Prehistoric and protohistoric archaeology of the most Ancient East is the

key to a correct interpretation of European prehistory. The latter in its early stage is mainly the history of imitation of oriental achievements or, at most, their adoption. The achievements themselves we know from the archaeology of the Orient." (Čajld 1954: 24–5). The "dogmatic orientalism" is still there.

The content of the preface which appeared in this translation was quite unexpected. In it Childe's thinking was in general approved! The preface was written by Academician Avdiev, a prominent orientalist. As an orientalist he found a way of making Childe's "dogmatic orientalism" (i.e. diffusionism) acceptable even from the Soviet point of view: he opposed it to europocentrism. The main value for the book he declared was its "correct conclusion that oriental peoples long before western ones created a number of cultural values, which in many respects influenced the development of western civilizations and not infrequently were even borrowed by western peoples" (Avdiev 1954: 6).

Thus, in just a few years (the first half of the 1950s) Russian readers became acquainted with the main works of Childe the diffusionist. But such works as *Man makes himself*, *What happened in history* and *Piecing together the past* were never translated.

The final explanations

Childe also visited the USSR in the year of Stalin's death, 1953. Soon further dramatic events occurred which were to mark a cardinal turning-point in the history of the country. In February 1956, six years after the annihilation of Marrism and three years after Stalin's death, Khruščov read his well known denunciation to the Twentieth Party Congress. The entire world of Marxism was shattered, and this was the beginning of the end of Communism. I shall not analyze the psychological trauma that Childe experienced, nor his attempts to place the blame for orthodox Marxism on Marrism, nor his subsequent shock and inner wretchedness. This has been written about elsewhere.

In spring 1956 Childe travelled to the USSR for the last time and visited Moscow and Leningrad. He was very eager to obtain manuscripts left by the late Kričevskij who had died in the siege of Leningrad (Childe still estimated Kričevskij's works highly!), but Kričevskij's widow, Kapošina, was startled, and, fearing defaming foreign connections, did not give them to him. This was a small disappointment, but it reinforced his general mood of bitterness and antipathy, and became the straw that broke the camel's back. These circumstances prompted Childe to look round him with the new eyes of a man who had experienced the fall of idols, first Marr and then Stalin. But it was very sad to feel himself Don Quixote and to see Dulcinea in all her squalor.

In his talks with his Soviet colleagues, Childe did not express his scepticism, except to Brjusov, because the moment Childe uttered a critical word Brjusov disgorged a much more critical tirade (Merpert has said he was present at their conversation in Moscow). In Leningrad, pausing a while on the banks of Neva by the entrance to the Institute of Archaeology and then on the Trinity Bridge, enjoying the view of Vasilij Island, admiring the Peter-and-Paul citadel, he said (according to Vsevolod Sorokin, then the Scholarly Secretary of the Institute): "There are more beautiful cities – I have seen Venice, Paris, Budapest. But a more beautiful place exists nowhere". And then he left.

Yet, back in London in December 1956, less than a year before his suicide, he wrote a letter to several prominent Soviet archaeologists in which he gave vent to his disillusion, bewilderment and grief. Professor Merpert, Dr Shilov, ex-Director of the Leningrad department of the Institute of Archaeology in the Academy of Sciences, and Professor Masson, now Director of the Petersburg Institute, have told me that the letter was sent personally to Artamonov in Leningrad, Arcikhovskij in Moscow and Efimenko in Kiev. This much is certain. With a copy found in Iessen's personal archives there was in indication that the letter had been addressed to Rybakov and Tolstov. Perhaps there were also other addressees. The letter was not preserved in Artamonov's archives. Merpert, then the Learned Secretary of the Moscow Institute, remembered Arcikhovskij, who was a very timid and loyal man, coming to his office, holding Childe's envelope in front of him by the corner with two fingers, in order not to leave fingerprints, and saying: "Vile letter! Probably he was forced to [write it]. Take it, if they need it in the Institute. I don't need it". Merpert said he translated it into Russian. Perhaps he was not the only translator.

In accordance with the customs of the period of the "Thaw", the letter did not go at once into the secret archives but was read in closed meetings (probably of party members) in Moscow and Leningrad. Masson was present at the Leningrad meeting (as the then secretary of Komsomol in the Institute). The letter was heard, taken into consideration, but of course not published. However, young archaeologists knew that such a letter had come. They remembered it and passed secretly made copies from hand to hand. One such copy (only the Russian translation) was received from Vsevolod Sorokin, the former Scholarly Secretary of the Leningrad Institute, by my friend Bočkarev; and from him it came to me. In search of the original text, Pletneva (the Chief Editor of *Sovetskaya Arkheologija*) asked, at my request, some old Moscow archaeologists and a typed English version was found in Merpert's archives – the same one that Arcikhovskij had given to him.* Merpert handed it to me and simultaneously to *Sovetskaja* (now *Rossijskaja Arkheologija*). The following quotations are taken from the original English text. There is no heading. The bull is taken by the horns:

---

* *Editorial note.* This is the original letter typed by Childe in London in December 1956 and reproduced in facsimile for the first time in this volume. It is now in the Childe archive at the Institute of Archaeology.

I have studied sympathetically Russian literature on prehistory since 1926. I appreciate fully such outstanding achievements as the recognition of artificial dwellings in the Upper Palaeolithic, the total excavations of whole Tripolye villages, Tolstov's observation at Kokcha III showing that not all double burials of male and female are necessarily contemporary and evidence for satî, Semeonov's study of traces of use on flint and bone implements, the successful preservation of the frozen relics from Pazyryk, etc. In English books and periodicals I have always emphasized the positive achievements of Soviet colleagues. But just for that reason I should like to confess here that I am profoundly disappointed.

In excavation technique Soviet archaeology falls far below the standards recognized in Britain, Czechoslovakia or even Germany. Of course I judge from publications. But it is the duty of an excavator to publish clear and large plans and sections showing every detail he can observe for the benefit of his colleagues at home and abroad".

Childe then gives a good scolding to his Soviet colleagues, dealing with each kind of monument separately:

In the excavation of barrows (Grabhügel, kurgans) I know no plan published since the Revolution so adequate as Gorodtsov's plan and section of the Odessa kurgan . . . Even that falls far short of the publication of van Giffen and his disciples in this country and elsewhere.

No systematic search seems to have been made under kurgans for features other than the actual burials . . .

The publication at least of domestic sites is still worse. No plans do I know of the houses so acutely recognized by Efimenko at Kostienki I at all! The tiny plans (without sections) of the "long houses" at Kostienki IV . . . and Pushkari . . . are quite unworthy and provoke scepticism. The "long house" might really be just a row of 12 . . . small round huts . . .

In later periods the number of zemlianky [underground dwellings – L. K.] is suspicious. Before 1940 the soil of Britain and Germany was also supposed to be pitted with "pit-dwellings" or Wohngruben. These have proved to be really silos or rubbish-pits . . . side by side with . . . large overground houses, supported by posts the sockets (Pfostenlocher) [sic! – L. K.] for which can always be recognized by an experienced excavator. Of course such houses have occasionally been identified in the USSR – e.g., by Briusov . . . [this may be the subject of the conversation with Brjusov referred to above – L. K.] or on sites of the Srubnaya or Andronovo cultures. But there must be more. . . . British, Danish, Dutch and German excavators (often aided by air-photographs, . . .) have discovered and planned ancient plough-furrows, field systems and cattle-enclosures . . . Are there any such from European Russia?

Finally the published sections through the ramparts of gorodishche [hill forts – L. K.] give little information . . .

Next Childe passes to the problems of relative and absolute chronologies:

For a relative chronology typology, uncontrolled by stratigraphy supplemented by distribution maps, is at best unreliable. . . . For an absolute chronology parallels in the historical civilizations of the Near East may provide a foundation. But the parallels must be exact . . .

In dating methods derived from the natural sciences Soviet archaeologists are also far behind. Thus "The pollen-analyses published from USSR are not easily comparable to those from the West Baltic or the United Kingdom . . ." Soviet archaeologists are also criticized for still using the old system of long chronology for the Bronze Age proposed by Montelius in 1903, whereas western and central European archaeologists long ago adopted the new, short one. Neither has convincing proof – they are "just guesses, and Soviet guesses may be as good as British or Czech" – but one needs to work in a single system in order to be able to compare sites. "Hancar in Das Pferd by treating the Russian and German dates as strictly comparable, reaches quite illegitimate conclusions . . . "

The last section of this dressing down is devoted to the notion of culture:

The reinstatement of the concept of culture among interpretative concepts I personally welcome. Still it seems to be used in the rather naïve manner adopted chiefly in Germany. . . . But a culture must of course be a recurrent assemblage of distinctive traits in different materials and revealing distinct aspects of human activity . . . But how do my Soviet colleagues define the katakombnaya kul'tura? Gorodtsov used the grave type. But what is Popova's criterion? . . . Are all the ceramic types she recognizes as katakombnaya at least sometimes found in katakomb graves? (That is are there some katakomby in her srednedneprovski group?). Do katakomby occur throughout the whole region attributed in her map to the katakombnaya kultura? . . . Maps showing distributions by shading or outlines are suitable instruments for vulgarization, not for additions to knowledge".

With these words the letter stops suddenly, as if broken off, with just the typed name, place and date: "V. Gordon Childe, The Athenaeum, London, SW1. 16/12/56".

One can imagine with what expressions these hard words were heard by the arrogant grandees of Soviet scholarly establishments who had declared for so long the superiority of Soviet scholarship that they believed in it themselves. This was a deafening box on the ear. Even now, 35 years later, there have been suggestions in Moscow that the letter may not be genuine – is it not a counterfeit?

The letter has no heading, no addressee(s), no introductory greeting and no signature. But the text is corrected by the same hand as addressed the envelope – the hand of Childe. And the genuineness of its content is

supported by the coincidence with what was written in a letter that Childe
wrote in August 1957, less than two months before his suicide, to Daniel as
the editor who had asked Childe to write a book, *The prehistory of Russia* (to
be published in the Ancient Peoples and Places Series).

I gather you're still hoping to get a book on Russian prehistory out of
me. But you won't . . . Even if one did explore the unpublished collections in remote museum magazines . . . I shouldn't find the evidence to
produce a coherent story that would convince me, for I don't believe it
yet exists. One cannot just enumerate a number of archaeological "facts"
in any old order; they must be set at least in a chronological frame. But
the relative and absolute chronology for the neo- and palaeometallic
stages is just hopelessly vague. The official Russian schemes are really
guesses that do not even attract, still less convince me. Passek's division
of Tripolye is terribly subjective and I see no reason why Tripolye A
(whatever it is) should be put nearer 3000 than 2000 BC. An equal
uncertainty affects the absolute dating of the Kuban culture . . . I don't
feel inclined to choose between such divergent guesses without convincing evidence. And I think to publish one guess, however often its
guesswork character be repeated, is positively harmful and misleading.
Yet the choice must be made in arranging the material for a book and
the arrangement is thus the assertion of one hypothesis that no account
of reservations will banish from the reader's mind . . . Until there be
evidence to support one well-grounded hypothesis on the main issues a
book on prehistoric Russia would be premature and misleading.

We may expect C-14 dates to resolve the major issues. But a summary
of the Russians' guesses, as though they were facts, *à la Hančar*, is worse
than useless. (Daniel 1958: 66–7)

Coincidences, including the remark on Hančar, are striking. When Daniel
published this letter in 1958, he added a challenge: "The comments which he
[Childe] wrote . . . on Russian prehistory are devastating. We hope they will
be answered, and our columns, no less than those of *The New Statesman and
Nation*, are wide open to Russian comment and criticism" (Daniel 1958: 67).
But the challenge remained without response, the columns waited in vain.
Russian archaeologists who already knew Childe's opinion kept silent, as if
they had got water in their mouths.

Perhaps the warnings of Childe were among the causes responsible for
Soviet archaeologists failing – up to now – to write a general book on the
prehistory of Russia, although in England such a book was eventually
published by Sulimirski in 1970 (and it was not a bad book, cf. Klejn 1974b).

Posthumous recognition

In 1958 an obituary of Childe, written by his traditional Soviet opponent Mongajt, appeared in *Sovetskaja Arkheologija*, the only archaeological journal published in Russia. Here for the first time the sacred truth was declared *urbi et orbi* that Childe was a Marxist. This was thoroughly substantiated. He was also a diffusionist, but Marxism and diffusionism no longer necessarily contradicted each other. They could now co-exist in Soviet archaeology. Of course Mongajt added a qualification:

> However, his views differ in many ways from the views of other Marxists, particularly from those of his colleagues in the USSR. Childe paid close attention to the development of Soviet archaeological thinking, sometimes criticizing us [the only hint at the existence of the final letter!], but also listening to our critiques. As the years passed the views of Childe and of Soviet archaeologists drew closer and closer together" (Mongajt 1958: 285).

This was the usual practice in the Soviet Union in relation to foreign Left-wing intellectuals. While he lives, one must beware of him: God knows what a trick he might play tomorrow, and your warm attestations may prove dangerous for you (in Soviet life political accusations were always retroactive and contagious). But a dead Marxist is certainly a good Marxist; his Marxist views remain Marxist forever. Can Childe be considered a Marxist forever?

As we have seen, there is no specific rejection of Marxism in the letters of Childe which have been cited. There is sharp criticism of some well known Soviet archaeologists, and, also criticism of the entire conduct of archaeological studies in the USSR. But the impressions of Glyn Daniel and Grahame Clark that Childe in the last period of his life rejected Marxism are probably not correct.

His statements in the essay that he sent to the Institute of Archaeology in London from Australia in 1957 (the so-called "Valediction") are not more radical in this respect. Indeed, in it he says that "universal laws of social development are far fewer and far less reliable than Marrists before 1950 thought" (Childe 1958a: 5). Clark made a characteristic mistake when he cited this passage; he wrote "Marxists" instead of "Marrists", but Childe was very careful not to mix these two notions. To Childe of the 1950s it is Marrism that "completely failed to explain the differences between one culture and another and indeed obliterated or dismissed as irrelevant the differences observed" (Childe 1958a: 6–7). There is no refutation of Marxism here, either subjective or objective. There is only bitter disappointment with Marr's extreme views. The essence of Marxism is not touched here. And it is not by chance that he reiterated in the "Retrospect", at the very end of his life, the phrase "even the Marrist perversion of Marxism" and the like (Childe 1958b: 72–3).

Perhaps if Childe really was no longer a Marxist, he would not have suffered such disappointment over the successes of Soviet scholarship. Among the causes of his decision to cease living (fear of illnesses and of medical operation, the prospect of his personal economic state worsening in retirement, some rejection of his scholarly conclusions), his general disillusionment with Soviet archaeology as a representative of Marxism is not the least important. The doubts as to Marxism itself might have come later. Communism has been conclusively wrecked in the past two years, and Marxism, its scholarly basis, is in deep crisis: a crisis that is connected with many personal tragedies, broken fates and departures from life.

To extend the idea of Trigger (1983), one could say: "If Childe were alive today" he would commit suicide again. He was a man of his time, the right man in a troublesome time. And this time is finished. In the new epoch which has set in there appears to be more and more place for Childe's everlasting achievements, and less and less place for the man himself. With admiration and sympathy we appreciate his great labours, his inexorable conscientiousness, and his tragic love.

Notes

1. As this volume was being despatched for printing, Professor Klejn found documents showing that this version of events is incorrect. He has now established that Latynin's manuscript, which had a similar title, disappeared after his arrest in 1935. Kruglov and Podgayetskij wrote *The clan society of the steppes of eastern Europe* independently in 1932–4 and it was printed before Latynin was arrested.

References

Arcikhovskij, A. V. 1949. Predislovie. In Čajld (Childe) 1949: 5–16.
Artamonov, M. I. 1947. Review of Childe's *Scotland before the Scots. Vestnik Leningradskogo Universiteta* 7, 111–21.
Avdiev, V. I. 1954. Predislovie. In Čajld (Childe) 1954: 5–18.
Bogaevskij, B. L. 1931. K voprosu o teorii migracij. *Soobščenija GAIMK* 8, 35–8.
Čajld (Childe), V. G. 1949. *Progress i arkheologija*. Moscow: Izdat. Inostrannaya Literatury.
1952. *U istokov Evropejskoj civilizacii*. Moscow: Izdat. Inostrannaya Literatury.
1954. *Drevnejšij Vostok v svete novykh raskopok*. Moscow: Izdat. Inostrannaya Literatury.
Childe, V. G. 1925(1957). *The dawn of the European civilization*, 6th edn. London: Kegan Paul, Trench, Trubner.
1930. New views on the relations of the Aegean and the North Balkans. *Hellenic Society, Journal* 50, 255–63.
1934. *New light on the most ancient East*. London: Kegan Paul, Trench, Trubner.
1940. Archaeology in the USSR. *Nature* 145, 110–11.
1942. Prehistory in the USSR. *Man* 42, 98–199, 100–3, 130–6.
1943. Archaeology in the USSR. *Man* 43, 4–9.
1944. Recent excavations on prehistoric sites in Soviet Russia. *Man* 44, 41–3.
1945a. Archaeology and anthropology in the USSR. *Nature* 156, 224–5.

1945b. *Progress and archaeology.* London: Watts.

1946a. The science of man in the USSR. *Man* **46**, 17–18.

1946b. *Scotland before the Scots.* London: Methuen.

1951. *Social evolution.* London: Watts.

1958a. Valediction. *Bulletin of the Institute of Archaeology, University of London* **1**, 1–8

1958b. Retrospect. *Antiquity* **32**, 69–74.

1979. Prehistory and Marxism. *Antiquity* **53**, 93–5.

Clark, J. G. D. 1976. Prehistory since Childe. *Bulletin of the Institute of Archaeology, University of London* **13**, 1–21.

Daniel, G. E. 1958. Editoral. *Antiquity* **32**, 65–8.

Klejn, L. S. 1974a. Kossinna im Abstand von vierzig Jahren. *Jahresschrift für mitteldeutsche Vorgeschichte* **58**, 7–55.

Klejn, L. S. 1974b. Review of Sulimirski's *Prehistoric Russia. Proceedings of the Prehistoric Society* **40**, 211–14.

Mongajt, A. L. 1951. Krizis buržuaznoj arkheologii. *Kratkie soobščenija* IIMK (Moscow) **40**, 3–15.

1952. Predislovie. In Čajld (Childe) 1952: 3–18.

1958. Gordon Čajld (1892–1957). *Sovetskaja Arkheologija* **3**, 284–7.

1973–6. *Arkheologija Zapadnoj Evropy.* Tt. I-II. Moskow: Nauka.

Sulimirski, T. 1970. *Prehistoric Russia: an outline.* London: John Baker.

Trigger, B. G. 1980. *Gordon Childe: revolutions in archaeology.* London: Thames & Hudson.

Trigger, B. G. 1983. If Childe were alive today. *Bulletin of the Institute of Archaeology, University of London* **19**, 1–20.

Discussion
CHAIRED BY PETER GATHERCOLE

Gathercole: A riveting, most moving paper, and a witty one.

Trigger: This letter is an amazing document and I want to thank you for bringing it to us. It has a thorough ring of authenticity to it; one does not have to see it with one's own eyes to believe it. It seemed to me from my own work that there is much about Childe and his relation to Marxism and his inner thoughts that is very hard to document. But I think that part of the crisis that comes out in this letter really goes back in his thinking to just before 1945, because this is the period when he says, in his autobiographical works, that he was re-studying Russian archaeological literature. What is very interesting is that, while he was doing so, two things happened: in his writings after this time he rarely says anything in praise of what Russian archaeologists are doing, and at the same time he begins this theoretical study of Marxism, which is no longer based on what Soviet archaeologists are doing but on the study of philosophical works. It is as if he is starting to build a new basis for a Marxist archaeology in succession to his earlier adoption of Soviet ideas. This is a kind of neo-Marxism, which seems to be Childe's effort to reinvent Marxism for himself, independently of what was going on in the Soviet Union. This is fascinating because, philosophically, and I think I could say anthropologically, his notions of cognitive maps and social knowledge were very productive and made an important intellectual contribution, even though people such as Anthony Wallace replicated them, apparently in total ignorance of Childe. The point is that, from then on, he rebuilt for himself a new, independent Marxism. So I wonder whether – and knowing that Childe often did not express his feelings – the judgement that is contained in the letter does not really date from that earlier wartime period and it was only at the end of his life that he got himself wound up enough, for whatever reason, to say what he actually felt.

Klejn: Yesterday, you said that Childe's mind was in bits and pieces. This is a very complex picture and our conference is trying to piece together Childe. So, even the more complex picture is of a sort of Marxism; but Soviet views changed frequently for many reasons, sometimes in the same direction as Childe's, sometimes in a different direction. And I think that, now that our eyes are open, other new documents will come to light. For example, recently many of E. H. Minns's letters to Russian archaeologists were found, and one of our young archaeologists has discovered in an archive the second of two volumes by Rostovtsev on Scythia and the Bosporus, which even Rostovtsev thought was lost. Only one volume ever appeared, and now the second will also be published.

Gathercole: It may be significant, in view of what Bruce has just said, that Childe's review of volume 1 of George Thomson's *Studies in ancient Greek society* (1949a), which came out in *Labour Monthly* (Childe 1949), was critical of orthodox Marxism, although he himself said there that he moved to a Marxist viewpoint by studying Russian periodicals *vis-à-vis* prehistory. Thomson was of course a member of the executive committee of the British Communist Party at the time, and it is interesting that the editor, Palme Dutt – amazingly – allowed Thomson to reply in the same number to Childe's criticisms (Thomson 1949b). What is interesting here is this bifurcation, which obviously had much earlier roots.

Could I perhaps also mention here an extraordinary opportunity which arose quite by accident? We have just put on a little exhibition about Childe in the Cambridge University Library, which those in Cambridge or visiting Cambridge might like to see (and this is not an ad.!). It includes a first edition of *How Labour governs* and a lot of other things, and while we were putting it up, an old colleague of mine from the Institute came up and produced a set of manuscripts for us. They are completely unknown lectures by Childe on Russian archaeology, given in Edinburgh in 1942. This is marvellous. I have only had them for about a week and Bruce has had a look at them; it is one of those extraordinary coincidences. According to a letter from Childe to Crawford, they were presented in the spring of 1942, which was only a few months after the Russians came into the Second World War.

Rowlands: I am interested in what you think of Childe's position in archaeology in Russia now. Is there likely to be future interest in his work?

Klejn: Childe is still a high authority of course, but it is very difficult to predict any archaeological attitudes because the whole of Russian archaeology is now in ferment. The most immediate task is how to survive, so little attention is paid to purely theoretical problems. The main questions for us are how to publish, how to finance expeditions, and how to continue subscribing to journals, etc.

Gathercole: May I ask you a question *vis-à-vis* what you were saying about the hidden meaning in the introduction to reviews of Childe's work? In the last few years, I have had some of the publications you referred to translated into English by, appropriately, an Australian colleague in Cambridge, who is not an archaeologist but has become very interested in them. As a linguistic specialist, she has said to me that she thought there were lots of hidden texts in these introductions. Was Childe, in your view, aware of this?

Klejn: Sometimes yes, sometimes no. Of course, he knew much more than he said, but I do not think he was conscious of the whole truth. The Soviet powers were very skilled in masking the reality in order to win the sympathy of left-wing intellectuals. I have written a book, *The phenomenon of Soviet archaeology* (1993), which contains a chapter on "The secret language of Soviet archaeologists". There are many methods of speaking – and of reading – truth between the lines. I have counted some 14 methods! The book is to be published in Russia, and in translation in Britain, Germany and Spain.

Gathercole: Can I ask to see the letter?

Klejn: Yes, of course. It is for the publisher of this volume.

Gathercole: Is it going to be in the book?

Harris: Yes, I hope so.

Klejn: It will also be published in *Rossijskaja Arkheologija* in the last issue of this year, but in a Russian translation, not the original text [*Editorial note:* in the event, the English version was published together with a Russian translation; see the Note that prefaces the facsimile of the letter in this volume].

Harris: Could I ask Leo to tell us a little more about the reaction to the letter? Even though it was largely hidden, but perhaps he could give us some idea of how far there was a differential reaction to different sections of the letter or whether it was just a shock reaction to the entire criticism at a general level?

Klejn: To assert now what the reaction was then is very difficult, of course. These meetings were at least partly protocoled ("fixed"), but because they were Party meetings the records of them have all been burned. It is now very difficult to find out about them.

Harris: But there are people who were there?

Klejn: Yes and I asked them. But it has become fabulous. Already there are legends and living myths. It is very difficult to get at the truth, but there are people who attended the meetings, such as Professor Masson in Leningrad and, I think, Professor Merpert in Moscow.

Harris: It just struck me, as you were describing the letter, that there would be certain sections of it that would be much more acceptable and much less hurtful than others.

Klejn: Yes, and some that were redundant also.

Bender: What strikes me very forcibly is the symmetry with which both the British and the Russians and, in fact, Childe in the letter, focus on practice rather than theory. But if you look at the British obituaries of Childe, where it is all about what a wonderful synthesizer he was, and that really the Marxism was a bit of an aberration. Then your wonderful account of how the Russians go back to *The dawn* and *The prehistory of European society* and say what a wonderful synthesizer he is, although we don't have to take too seriously some of his theoretical, rather bourgeois viewpoints. I believe that he remained a Marxist, it is *very* striking that there is not a single criticism launched at a theoretical level: that it is all at the level of practice. As you have said yourself, he was very uncomfortable with Soviet theory and yet I wonder why it is that in that letter the whole theoretical issue is so totally ignored?

Klejn: It is striking but there is no solution.

Bender: And you have no solution?

Klejn: No.

EDITOR'S COMMENT: After this discussion took place Professor Klejn gave me a note suggesting three possible answers to Dr Bender's question. Either (a) Childe had no significant objections to orthodox Soviet Marxism; or (b) he thought that Soviet scholars were too rigid in their orthodox views to respond to argument; or (c) he did not wish to concentrate on irreconcilable differences of view and wanted to offer criticism as a friend not an enemy.

References

Childe, V. G. 1949. Marxism and the Classics. *Labour Monthly* 31, 250–3.

Klejn, L. S. 1993. *The phenomenon of Soviet archaeology* (in Russian). St Petersburg: Farn.

Thomson, G. 1949/1955. *Studies in ancient Greek society*. Vol. 1: *The prehistoric Aegean* (1949); Vol. 2: *The first philosophers* (1955). London: Lawrence & Wishart.

Wallace, A. F. C. 1961. *Culture and personality*. New York: Random House

Facsimile of a letter dated 16 December 1956 from Gordon Childe to Soviet Archaeologists

Note from the Editor

The existence of the letter reproduced here was revealed to Western archaeologists by Professor Leo Klejn on 9 May 1992 during the Conference. In his paper in this volume he reports what he has been able to discover about the letter's history following its initial arrival in Leningrad. He gave the original to me after delivering his paper, and it is now in the Childe archive at the Institute of Archaeology, University College London. A Russian translation of the letter, with the original English version, was published in *Rossijskaja Arkheologija* in late 1992 (Part 4: 184–9), accompanied by a note "On the publication of V. G. Childe's letter" by N. I. Merpert (ibid: 189–96). This is the first time the original English version has been published in the West. The typescript of the letter and the style of Childe's hand corrections are identical to those of other letters typed by Childe which are in the archive at the Institute.

FROM GORDON CHILDE TO SOVIET ARCHAEOLOGISTS

I have studied sypathetically Russian literature on prehistory since 1926. I appreciate fully such outstanding achievements as the recognition of artificial dwellings in the Upper Palaeolithic, the total excvation of whole Tripolye villages, Tolstov's observation at Kokcha III showing that not all double burials of male and female are necessarily contemporary and evidence for satî, Semeonov's study of traces of use on flint and bone implements, the successful preservation of the frozen relics from Pazyryk, etc. In English books and periodicals I have always emphasized the positive achievements of Soviet colleagues. But just for that reason I should like to confess here that I am profoundly disappointed.

In excavation technique Soviet archaeology falls far below the standards recognized in Britain, Czechoslovakia or even Germany. Of course I judge from publications. But it is the duty of an excavator to publish clear and large plans and sections showing every detail he can observe for the benefit of his colleages at home and abroad. It has often happened that another investigator can discover significant features thus presented though they were not understood by the excavator; for instance in 1938 Bersu was able to recognize as granaries and hay-racks some groups of posts, apparently meaningless but faithfully recorded in plans twenty years old of the Glastonbury Lake Village. Indeed from my own old plans in the light of later experience I have sometimes been able to detect features that I had been unable to interpret at the time of the excavation.

In the excavation of barrows(Grabhügel, kurgans) I know no plan published since the Revolution so adequate as Gorodtsov's plan and section of the Odessa kurgan(Otchet Imp.Ross. Istorichesk. Muzea v Moskve za 1915 g.) Even that falls far short of the publications of van Giffen and his disciples in this country and elsewhere.

No systematic search seems to have been made under kurgans for features other than the actual burials such as an encircling ditch, a ring of posts or similar structures; these are seldom mentioned explicitly and very rarely shown in plans and sections. Yet such things throw much light at least on the ideology of the kurgan-builders as the work of van Giffen in Holland and of Fox in Wales has shown.

The publication at least of domestic sites is still worse.
No plans do I know of the houses so acutely recognized by Efimenko
at Kostienki I at all! The tiny plans (without sections) of the
"long houses" at Kostienki IV(K.S.,IV,1940,37) and Pushkari(K.S.
VII,1940,82) are quite unworthy and provoke scepticism. The"long
house" might really be just a row of 12 or 8 small round huts
like those of Gagarino and Buryat,dug perhaps in consecutive
years but overlapping!

In later periods the number of Wohng zemlianky is suspicious.
Before 1940 the soil of Britain and Germany was also supposed to
be pitted with "pit-dwellings" or Wohngruben. These have proved
to be really silos or rubbish-pits(Kornspeicher or Abfallgruben)
side by side with(gleichzeitig mit) large overground houses,
supported by posts the sockets(Pfostenlocher) for which can
always be recognized by an experienced excavator. Of course
such houses have occasionally been identified in the U.S.S.R.-
e.g., by Briusov(MIA,20,1951) or on sites of the Srubnaya or
Andronovo cultures. But there must be more. In particular
Tripolye houses,if not actually raised on piles as the models
suggest,must have been supported by a frame of posts such as
Laszlo found in 1912 under typical ploshchadki at Erösd(Ariusd)
(Dolgozatok az Erdélyi Nemzeti Muzeum II(Koloszvar-Cluj,1914).

British Danish,Dutch and German excavators(often aided by
air-photographs,taken at the right season,the correct time of
day or the appropriate angle) have discovered and planned ancient
plough-furrows,field systems and cattle-enclosures and thus
revealed many details of the rural ecomomy (?selskoe khozyastwo)
from prehistoric to medieval times, Are there any such from
European Russia?

Finally the published sections through the ramparts of
gorodishche give little information. Well-conducted excavations
in England and Germany have disclosed the timber revetments
that once supported really formidable ramparts of which the
postholes or foundations trenches alone survive.Very refined
excavation even reveals tansverse tie-beams in the wall as at
Wittnauer Horn(G.Bersu)

For a relative chronology typology, uncontrolled by stratigraphy supplemented by distribution maps, is at best unreliable. When
applied to decorative motives or pot-forms it is particularly
suspect. Briusov has conclusively shown that the last "stage" of
Passek's Tripolye sequence is not a stage at all chronologically,
but a local spatial phenomenon. Only more detailed distribution
maps can show whether other "stages"- especially Passek's A - be not
really also local styles. Metal tools and weapons may provide a
reliable series that is really chronological provided there are
plenty of rich closed finds, ideally grave groups. This condition is
seldom satisfied save in Cis-Caucasia (?Zakavkaza) where Yessen's
fivefold division seems well based (SA. XII, 1950, 157 → 188)

For an absolute chronology parallels in the historical civilizations of the Near East may provide a foundation. But the parallels
must be exact. And only if barbarian types appear in correspomding
strata in the Orient and Aegean can a precise synchronims be claimed
Now the axes and daggers from Usla Usatova are not exactly like any
dateable Aegean or Oriental types — the daggers in fact are very
unusual: the nearest, but still not exact parallels come from South
Spain (Los Millares) and South France and are undatable. No inference
at all as to the closing phase of Tripolye could be drawn from them!
The Maikop and Novosvobodnaya types do agree well with Mesopotamian
and Hissar III forms. But the former were used with little change
from say 2500, to 1200 B.C. and Hissar III may be dated anywhere
between 2300 and 1500! To, appeal to Seima for a date for the
Borodino hoard (Kritsova-Grakova, Bessarabskii Klad) is surely
ignotum ;per ignotius? Analogies between the stone axes and the
bronze axes of Faskau type would be more significant, but even
Faskau is not well dated? On the other hand the hammer-pins from
the Royal Tombs of Alaca Höyük are too like the Pontic-Caucasian
specimens to be accidental (see especially Hamit Zubeyr Kosay,
Alaca Höyük Kazisi (Turk Tarih Kurum Yayinlarindan V, 5, Ankara, 1951)
pl. CXXXV, 2) As the type is much commoner in the USSR than in
Turkey and so may rank as Pontic in origin it would give a terminum
ante quem → "before 2000 B.C."- for the transition from
drevneyamno to katakombnaya period!

Russian use of natural chronology d̸i̸v̸e̸r̸g̸e̸ does not diverge from "western" usage, but only from the latest western usage. Czech, English, French, German and Italian geologists now a̸c̸c̸p̸t̸ admit a fairly long genial"interstadial2(WI-II) interrupting the last(Wurm) ice age. The nizhni horizont at Kostienki I and Iskaya would fit in much better in W₁ - II than in Riss→Wurm(cf?Efimenko,Pervobytnoe Obshchestvo 1953,204,330)

The pollen-analyses published from USSR are not easily comparable to those from the West Baltic or the United Kingdom. The refinements introduced by Jessen,Iversen,Troels→Smith in Denmark and by Godwin in England (counting more grains,including herbs and grasses as well as trees,etc.) are not represented in the pollen diagrams, published in Russian archaeological periodicals. The zones defined by these improved methods have now been provisionally"dated"by C 14. Zone IV(Pre→Boreal→ circa 7500 B.C.(Clark,Star Carr);Zone V(Early Boreal) c.6300 etc.

Soviet archaeologists seem to take the absolute dates for the Bronze Age given by Montelius about 1903 ignoring the fact that in the interval the Egyptian and "esopotamian dates on which they were based have been drastically deflated. British,Czech and Danish pre-historians have always preferred much lower figures and Germans and Swedes have recently fallen into line. From the old high dates for the beginning of the Bronze Age Russian prehistorians seem to have reckoned back by a sort of extrapolation that has been unfashionable in the West since 1918(save in Nazi Germany) and reached high dates for the Neolithic. Of course the low British,Czech and Danish systems are also just guesses and Soviet guesses may be as good as British or Czech. But at the moment the two systems allow of no comparisons of age between sites say in the Ukraine and in North Germany. Hancar in Das Pferd by treating the Russian and German dates as strictly comparable reaches quite illegitimate conclusions; there is no evidence to show whether Dummer or Ossarn is earlier or later than Usbkova. Efimenko's comparisons between earlymNeolithic sites in Ukraine and Maglemose on the Baltic are unconvincing. The Maglemosean is well dated in terms of pollen zones and is represented by abundant and varied material relics the development of which can be followed round the North Sea from Zone IV at Star Carr(Yorkshire) through the classical Maglemosean of Zones V-VI to survivals in Zone VIII and indeed in the folk-culture of the Baltic lands today. Till a comparable wealth of really distinctive types, naturally dated by pollen, geology or C 14, be found in the Ukraine or South Russia, the priority of these areas will seem unlikely.

The reinstatement of the concept of culture among interpretative concepts I personally welcome. Still it seems to be used in the rather naive manner adopted chiefly in Germany. In Germany between 1921 and 1945 every newly-found local variety of neolithic pottery was made into a new"culture" even though nothing else was regularly associated with the novel pottery. But a culture must of course be a recurrent assemblage of distinctive traits in different materials and reveal- ing distinct aspects of human activity — tools and weapons, house-plans and burial rites, personal ornaments and decorative patterns. But how do my Soviet colleages define the katakombnaya kul'tura? Gorodstov used the grave type. But what is Popova's criterion?(SA., XXII, 1955, 21f Are all the ceramic types she recognizes as katakomnaya at least sometimes found in katakamb graves(That is are there some Katakomby in her srednedneprovski group?). Do kaktakomby occur thoughout the whole region attributed in her map to the katakombnaya kultura?(Ris.5 p.41) I know katakomby on the Volga(Rau, Hockergräber der Volgasteppe, 48 & 52) assigned by Popova to the Poltavka kul'tura. But Poltavka pottery, though normally found in yamy does not diverge from the standard more than the other variants she shows in her Fig?9. There are also katakomby near Odessa, on the Kuban Kuban-Terek and even in Daghestan, outside the boudaries of her province. Why not give maps showing the distribution of katakomby, katakombnaya daggers, hammer pins cranial deformation, etc. by points for each kurgan or kurgan-cemetery (as by Foss, MIA., 29) That would show what types really hang together. Maps showing distributions by shadings or outlines are suitable instruments for vulgarization, not for additions to knowledge.

V.Gordon Childe,

16/12/56 The Athenaeum, London, SW.I

Childe the evolutionist
A perspective from Nuclear America

KENT V. FLANNERY

This paper is dedicated to the memory of Emilio Choy (1915–76)

In the course of this conference we have heard about Childe the social theorist, Childe the Marxist and pacifist, Childe the arbiter of scientific ethics, and Childe the synthesizer. I would now like to consider Childe the evolutionist, particularly with regard to the evolution of New World civilizations. When I was a graduate student working on Near Eastern archaeology under Robert J. Braidwood, I heard a great deal about V. Gordon Childe. Part of what I heard, of course, was that his "oasis-propinquity hypothesis" wouldn't work as an explanation for the origins of agriculture in the Near East (Braidwood & Howe 1960: 7). Apart from this, I heard great praise and respect for the man who had written *New light on the most ancient East* (Childe 1934) and *Man makes himself* (Childe 1936). There had been no overarching theory for the early Near East before Childe. He had taken a mass of data, collected almost entirely by others, and put it into a framework of successive revolutions, technological stages, and criteria for civilization.

North American archaeology

Once I had moved into New World archaeology, I heard much less about Childe. Although he had incorporated some New World cultures into his scheme, he knew (and cared) much less about them and tended consistently to underrate their level of development. Consider, for example, his comment that "the minimum definition of a city . . . will be substantially reduced and impoverished by the inclusion of the Maya (Childe 1950: 9), and his complete misunderstanding of the content of Maya writing (see below). Within the New World, it is perhaps among North American archaeologists that Childe's impact is least felt. One reason, surely, is that North American societies never went through an urban revolution. We have one Southwest US archaeologist who considers himself a Marxist (McGuire 1992), but most Americans using a Marxist approach have Old World interests (Gilman 1984, Kohl 1984). Our most complete treatment of Childe is by a Canadian who has worked in both the New and Old Worlds (Trigger 1980).

It is not only the pre-state, pre-urban condition of native North American societies, however, that has discouraged Marxist approaches. A contributing variable is the fact that US archaeologists, in contrast to their European counterparts, are not sophisticated at separating Marxist *theory* from Marxist *politics*. For most US veterans of the Cold War, the fall of a Marxist government is a sign that Marxism as a framework for historical analysis is also flawed. Most probably share the view of our noted humorist A. Whitney Brown. When the Berlin Wall fell, eastern Europe went democratic, and Leningrad reverted to St Petersburg, Brown (1991) remarked: "Who would have thought that the fatal flaw of Marxism would be that there's no money in it?".

Latin American archaeology

In Latin America, where there were several urban revolutions, the story is quite different. For many Latin American universities, there is no theory but Marxist theory. At the Escuela Nacional de Antropologia in Mexico City, one gifted archaeology student joked to me, "we have six courses on theory. All are on Marxist theory." It was therefore no surprise that in July of 1986, on the 50th anniversary of the publication of *Man makes himself*, a colloquium to honor Childe was held in Mexico City; the resultant volume was edited by Linda Manzanilla (1988). In Peru there are, indeed, competing theories, but none so respected as Marxism, rooted as it is in the tradition of such national heroes as Mariategui. Such distinguished Peruvian theorists as Luis Guillermo Lumbreras (1974) and Emilio Choy (1972) have interpreted the Inca empire in Marxist terms, and in their writings Childe holds a special place. I believe that Choy (1960) was the first Peruvian to apply the expression "Neolithic revolution" to the Andes. I first met Choy in 1968, and I remember my colleague Ramiro Matos telling him that I had recently placed Mexico's Neolithic revolution in a systems-theory framework (Flannery 1968). "Good," said Choy, "systems theory is the closest thing to the dialectic".

Childe and Nuclear America

In a paper of this length, one cannot cover everything Childe wrote. I therefore propose to limit myself to two topics: Childe's concept of Neolithic and Urban Revolutions, and the ten criteria for civilization given in his 1950 article in *The Town Planning Review* (Childe 1950). As Bruce Trigger emphasized at this conference, evolution for Childe was what *actually happened* in prehistory, not some abstract theory. I will therefore look briefly at what actually happened in Mesoamerica and the Andes, and indicate how we might agree or disagree with Childe's ideas today. Among other things, I will argue that there was another revolution, unrecognized by Childe, that needs to be interposed between Neolithic and Urban. I suggest that that revolution was "out of focus" for Childe because of his intense concentration on technology and the mode of production of food. I will also suggest that he left one of the most important variables of higher social evolution off his famous list of ten criteria for civilization. Thanks to comments by John Mulvaney and Bruce Trigger at this conference, I believe I know why.

The Neolithic Revolution

The moment we turn to the Neolithic Revolution in the Andes, we see that it was a much more complex process than Childe had imagined. Childe saw the life of the hunter–gatherer as "savagery" – nomadic, without villages. The Neolithic farmer, on the other hand, had achieved "barbarism" – permanent settlement, a new level of population density, and above all the potential for surplus (Childe 1950). But there were in fact three pathways to Neolithic life in the Andes: one in the highlands, one on the tropical eastern slopes, and one on the desert coast. In the highlands of Junin and Ayacucho – native home of the wild potato, oca, olluco, masua, and other potential root crops – people remained semi-nomadic cave-dwellers even after the domestication of native Andean camelids (MacNeish et al. 1983, Rick 1980). Here the Neolithic was slow to develop, just as it was slow to develop in highland Mexico. In the latter area, foragers remained semi-nomadic for thousands of years after they had brought bottle gourds, squash, beans, chile peppers, and even maize under cultivation (MacNeish 1964, Flannery 1973).

On the desert coast of Peru, on the other hand, marine resources permitted relatively large and permanent settlements even before agriculture was well established (Moseley 1975). Fishing and shell-fishing, combined with plant collection and the hunting of sea and land mammals, facilitated the transition from "savagery" to "barbarism" before the appearance of pottery and with only the most meagre evidence of cultivars (Lanning 1967a, Bonavia 1991). Villages of circular houses with whale-rib roof supports appeared atop extensive shell mounds at Chilca (Donnan 1964); huts with cobblestone foundations appeared at Huaca Prieta (Bird & Hyslop 1985). Some of the shell mounds on the coast of Peru, such as Ancon (Lanning 1967b), are as large as Near Eastern tells such as Musiyan and Nineveh. And these early settlements further undermine Childe's "oasis-propinquity hypothesis," since they occur on a coast where 4mm of annual rainfall is considered average. In an environment already that arid, "post-Pleistocene desiccation" would hardly have been noticed. While some of the early Andean coastal settlements produced monumental architecture in pre-pottery times, there is no reason to believe that society was anything but egalitarian at that period. Indeed, a recent analysis of the spectacular pre-pottery site of El Paraiso finds that it was probably a large egalitarian community, nucleated for the purpose of irrigating cotton but largely sustained by marine resources (Quilter et al. 1991).

The "Rank Revolution"

What happened next in the Andes and Mesoamerica was just as "revolutionary" as the origins of food production: the leap from an egalitarian society to one with hereditary inequality, regional civic-ceremonial centers, loss of village autonomy, and lavish use of manpower in the construction of public buildings. I will call this "the Rank Revolution," and suggest that it was out of focus for Childe because it involved changes in *ideology* and *social relationships* rather than the *means of production*. Childe made it very clear in his *Town Planning Review* article (Childe 1950) that the "technique of obtaining food [was used] to distinguish the consecutive stages termed savagery and barbarism" and that "the density of population is determined by the food supply which in turn is limited by natural resources, the techniques for their exploitation, and the means of transport and food preservation available." For Childe, "social division of labor" was impossible at the stages of savagery and barbarism "save those rudiments imposed by age and sex".

But between 1800 BC and AD 300 in Peru, and between 1200 BC and AD 150 in Mexico, we see the rise of "chiefdoms" or "rank societies." These new societies did not necessarily produce food differently from their Neolithic predecessors, but many used raiding or simple warfare to enforce tribute from outside their local resource sphere; they also supported craft specialists of high quality. Their great revolution lay not in a new way of producing food, but in a new ideology in which chiefly individuals and commoners had separate genealogical origins. That ideology justified the demands of greater output and productivity made by elite individuals and carried out by lower-status individuals. Such ideologies do not characterize egalitarian societies, who generally have leveling mechanisms to prevent society from being divided into elite and commoner. Among some Pueblo Indian societies of the southwestern US, for example, families who were able to accumulate more luxury goods, store more surplus, and establish more ostentatious life styles often faced accusations of witchcraft and perhaps even expulsion from the community. The Rank Revolution overcame such leveling mechanisms by rationalizing the perquisites of the elite.

Surplus figured importantly in Childe's evolutionary framework, but he seemed to see it as the logical consequence of better technology, which in turn made inegalitarian society inevitable. Many of today's New World archaeologists, on the contrary, would see Neolithic people as "satisfizers" for whom there was no incentive to produce surplus. The challenge, as Sahlins (1972) has pointed out, is "to get people to work more, or more people to work." Many New World archaeologists do not believe that this was likely to happen until there was an elite to command it. The Rank Revolution produced some of the most spectacular sites and public works in Nuclear America. Whether we are speaking of Complex A at La Venta in Mexico, with its earthen pyramids and buried serpentine pavements (Drucker et al. 1959), or the stone masonry temple of Chavin de Huantar in Peru, with its Great Image and labyrinthine galleries (Lumbreras & Amat 1965-6), the scale of corvée labor and monumental construction exceeds anything seen before hereditary inequality arose.

It is at this stage of cultural evolution that we come face to face with the variable Childe left out of his scheme: warfare. Childe, as both Trigger and Mulvaney have told us at this conference, was a pacifist. He saw warfare as a social ill – something that destroyed surplus, that crucial component of Childe's evolutionary model. Hence he could not see that warfare, long considered a destroyer of complex societies, was also one of the factors creating complex societies (Marcus 1992a, 1992b). But evidence for armed conflict, raiding, and terrorism is everywhere in Nuclear America at the rank society or "chiefdom" level of evolution. From Cerro Sechin on the north coast of Peru, with its graphic carvings of trophy heads, enemies quartered and disemboweled (Tello 1956, Samaniego et al. 1985), to the fortification walls and defensible locations of Late Formative sites in Mexico's Valley of Oaxaca (Elam 1989), or the carved scenes of decapitation in Chiapas (Norman 1973), it is clear that rank societies were violent societies.

Why are today's New World archaeologists so much more interested in the "chiefdom" stage of evolution than Childe was? For one thing, it is not necessarily in the mode of production that chiefdoms differ from the egalitarian societies that preceded them; hence Childe might not have seen them as significantly different. It is also the case that New World chiefdoms are so flamboyant, and shine so brightly in the archaeological record, that they cannot be ignored. It is far more difficult to identify early rank societies in the areas of the Old World that Childe knew best. In Mesopotamia, Egypt, and the Indus Valley, such an evolutionary stage seems to have been less flamboyant than the Olmec and Chavin cultures of the New World, and to have moved relatively rapidly to urban civilizations that were much more spectacular. Further setting the New World apart is the fact that some regions seem to have "plateaud" at the chiefdom level, so that our earliest European accounts of those regions describe chiefdoms and not states. In Panama, Colombia, and the southeastern US, the earliest Europeans found spectacular rank societies whose accounts have profoundly influenced New World archaeology. For Childe, such societies were only the prologue to his second revolution.

The Urban Revolution

There was indeed an Urban Revolution in Nuclear America, but it grew out of the rank societies mentioned above rather than Neolithic villages, and warfare continued to be one of the variables shaping its growth. Monte Alban in the Valley of Oaxaca may have been Mexico's first truly urban center (Blanton 1978), followed at no great interval of time by Teotihuacan in the Basin of Mexico, Mesoamerica's largest early city (R. Millon 1981). At its peak, Teotihuacan covered $25\,km^2$, while Monte Alban never exceeded $6.5\,km^2$.

Wari, in the Peruvian province of Ayacucho, seems to have been an urban center sprawling over several square kilometers and characterized by a high level of craft specialization (Isbell & McEwan 1991). Even the secondary centers of the Wari state, provincial capitals below Wari, were urban by Old World standards. For example, Pikillaqta near Cuzco (McEwan 1984) and Cajamarquilla in the Rimac Valley of the Peruvian coast (Stumer 1954) consist of walled compounds, plazas, alleys, and public buildings covering an area as large as that of most major Uruk or protoliterate sites in Mesopotamia. By AD 1100–1400, a Chimu state with its $20\,km^2$ urban capital at Chan Chan, near Trujillo, stretched 1,000 km from north to south along the Peruvian coast. Chan Chan's rulers lived in huge adobe-walled compounds which, like the so-called "labyrinth of Knossos", contained hundreds of storage facilities and quarters for an estimated 26,000 artisans (Moseley & Day 1982).

Childe's ten criteria for urban civilization

Having looked briefly at the Neolithic and Urban revolutions in Nuclear America – and having interposed a Rank Revolution between them – let us now look at the ten criteria for urban civilization proposed by Childe in his *Town Planning Review* article. What would a New World perspective on these ten criteria tell us?

1. Childe says that early cities were densely populated, although some may have had populations as small as 7,000 persons. For Nuclear America, we might argue that the figure should be lowered to 5,000 persons – low by twentieth-century standards, but not by the standards of medieval Europe.
2. Childe tells us that, while some urban dwellers may have been farmers, many were non-food producers. We agree, but would point out that the percentage of non-food producers in ancient New World cities was probably quite variable. For example, craft specialists at Teotihuacan may have been more numerous than those at Monte Alban (Flannery & Marcus 1983: 161–6).
3. Primary producers, Childe argues, paid tithes or taxes to the state. This was true of Nuclear America, and was in fact one of the sources of stress leading to armed conflict between urban capitals and their hinterlands.
4. For Childe, the monumental buildings of urban civilization "concentrate social surplus". This view is consistent with Childe's position that surplus

was the great creator of early states. New World archaeologists, particularly Andeanists, would probably argue that public buildings "flaunted the manpower at the disposal of chiefs and kings". Pointing to the marked adobe bricks used to build the Huaca del Sol on the Peruvian coast (Hastings & Moseley 1975), which indicate that different work gangs kept account of the bricks they contributed, Andeanists might argue that it was *labor*, not material surplus, that each ruler was concentrating.

5. In urban civilization, Childe argues, there was "a ruling class exempt from manual tasks". New World specialists would agree – unless you consider leading armies into battle to be a "manual task". But Childe defines his ruling class on the basis of concentration of surplus; New World archaeologists might see it as defined ideologically, genealogically, and socially (Marcus 1992b), with surplus simply falling under its command.

6. Urban civilizations, says Childe, had systems of record keeping and practical sciences. This is as true for the New World as the Old. For example, the Andean system of tying knots in cords called *quipu* (Ascher & Ascher 1981) was the New World counterpart for the accounts kept on cuneiform tablets by Mesopotamian scribes.

7. The invention of writing (or scripts), Childe argues, enabled "leisured clerks" to elaborate arithmetic, geometry, and astronomy. Here we come to a criterion that could have been left off Childe's list. Andean civilizations had no writing at all, only the record-keeping knotted cords mentioned above. Teotihuacan in the Basin of Mexico, urban capital of Mesoamerica's largest early state, had no writing except for what appear to be short glyphic captions – possibly names or titles – for human figures depicted in murals (C. Millon 1988).

Moreover, even in the case of the ancient Maya – who did have a complex hieroglyphic writing system, linked to the spoken language – Childe's tendency to think in terms of evolving science and technology caused him to misunderstand New World writing. In his *Town Planning Review* article he illustrates the Leyden Plate, a Classic Maya jade plaque incised with hieroglyphs (Childe 1950: Fig. 16). Using this inscribed jade as an example, Childe (1950: 14) says that the Maya calendar made possible "correct determination of the tropic year", and that the creation of a calendar enabled rulers to "regulate successfully the cycle of agricultural operations."

We should perhaps not to be too hard on Childe for this, for in 1950 a great many archaeologists (including Mayanists) thought that most Maya inscriptions were centered on the calendar and astronomy. Understandably, therefore, Childe's concern with technology, surplus, and the mode of production led him to believe that the Maya calendar was about agriculture. Today we can read the whole of the Leyden Plate (Marcus 1976), and we know that neither it nor any other Maya inscription carved in stone deals with the scheduling of agriculture in the tropic year.

The top 7 lines of the Leyden inscription give elapsed time in units of 400 years, 20 years, single years, months, and days since August 11. 3114 BC, the starting date of the Maya calendar. That elapsed time ends at a date when a ruler, whose name is given in line 11, was inaugurated – probably at the city of Tikal in Guatemala, whose emblem glyph appears to be given in line 12. According to Joyce Marcus (personal communication), the inscription can be roughly translated, "The ruler 'Bird–Sky' was inaugurated at Tikal on September 17, AD 320" (Fig. 1).

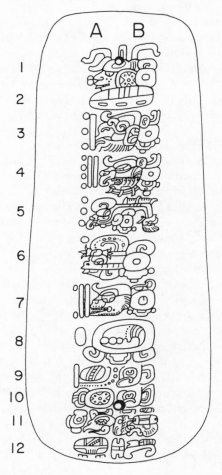

Figure 1 The Leyden plate
This inscription was used by Childe (1950: Fig. 16) as an example of Maya calendrics. Because of his focus on surplus, Childe assumed that the Maya calendar was designed to calculate the tropical year for agricultural purposes. In fact, the calendrics on the Leyden Plate refer to the date of a ruler's inauguration (see text). (Redrawn from Marcus 1976: Fig. 11.)

Maya inscriptions in stone had nothing to do with agriculture. Like Egyptian hieroglyphic inscriptions on stone, they consisted of political propaganda related to royal families – their conquests, royal marriages, genealogies, life crises, and reigns (Marcus 1992b). Childe not only misunderstood Maya writing, he also underestimated Maya civilization, as in his already-mentioned comment that "the minimal definition of a city . . . will be substantially reduced and impoverished by the inclusion of the Maya" (Childe 1950: 9). Perhaps he may be excused because in 1950, many authors believed that Maya cities were "vacant ceremonial centers" (Thompson 1954, Morley & Brainerd 1956). Today we know that Maya cities like Tikal (Haviland 1970), Calakmul (Folan 1992), and Copan (Fash 1991) were true urban centers with dense populations and thousands of structures.

8. Urban civilization, says Childe, gave a new direction to artistic expression – "naturalistic art." Archaeologists working in Nuclear America might phrase it differently. They might say that what was new was "state art", often involving an official style whose content was a form of political propaganda.

9. Childe sees "foreign trade" as a major activity for urban civilization. New World archaeologists would agree, but might also point out that long-distance trade had been important even before urbanism.

10. The city, says Childe, had a population whose organization was based "on residence rather than kinship". We understand Childe's point here and are sympathetic: in many urban melting pots, neighborhoods were defined by a shared profession rather than common ancestry. But given the presence of large kin-based units such as the Aztec *calpulli* and the Inca *ayllu*, New World archaeologists today would say that urban organization was based both on residence and on kinship.

Finally, given our discussion above, we would say that Childe could have dropped writing from his set of ten criteria, and substituted warfare.

Conclusion

Given these revisions of Childe's scheme – the addition of a third revolution and the modification of some of his criteria for urban civilization – how would we summarize his lasting contribution to the archaeology of Nuclear America? Marxist archaeologists in Latin America will always remember Childe as one of the first writers to put the archaic state in a context of mode of production, concentration of power in the hands of a few, and the growth of technology and surplus. United States archaeologists, while largely employing different explanatory frameworks, will acknowledge that he tried to do for surplus what Leslie White (1959) tried to do for energy: to use it as the variable by which evolutionary change could be monitored.

Most of all, perhaps, we will remember him as the man who made order out of archaeological chaos. From a mass of unconnected data, the greater part of it collected by others, he produced a framework of successive revolutions and technological stages that have provided us with food for discussion for more than half a century. It hardly matters that some details of Childe's scheme don't fit the current Nuclear American data. What matters is that Childe had a vision of evolution at a time when other archaeologists had only chronology charts.

References

Ascher, Marcia & Robert Ascher 1981. *Code of the Quipu: a study in media, mathematics and culture.* Ann Arbor: University of Michigan Press.

Bird, Junius B. & John Hyslop 1985. The Preceramic excavations at Huaca Prieta, Chicama Valley, Peru. *Anthropological Papers* **62**(1). New York: American Museum of Natural History.

Blanton, Richard E. 1978. *Monte Alban: settlement patterns at the ancient Zapotec Capital.* New York: Academic Press.

Bonavia, Duccio 1991. Perú: hombre e historia. De los orígenes al siglo XV. Lima: Ediciones Edubanco.

Braidwood, Robert J. & Bruce Howe 1960. *Prehistoric investigations in Iraqi Kurdistan.* Studies in Ancient Oriental Civilization 31. Chicago: University of Chicago Press.

Brown, A. Whitney 1991. Editorial comments during "Weekend Update", *Saturday Night Live.* New York: NBC Television.

Childe, V. Gordon 1934. *New light on the most ancient East.* London: Kegan Paul & Trench.

1936. *Man makes himself.* London: Watts & Co.

1950. The Urban Revolution. *The Town Planning Review* **21**(1), 3–17.

Choy, Emilio 1960. La Revolucion Neolitica y los origenes de la civilizacion Peruana. *Antiguo Peru: Espacio y Tiempo,* 149–97. Lima: Editorial Juan Mejla Baca.

1972. Estructuras de amortiguacion y lucha de clases en el sistema esclavista Incaico. *Proceedings of the 40th International Congress of Americanists,* Vol. 2, E. Cerulli (ed.), 511–13. Genova: Tilgher.

Donnan, Christopher B. 1964. An early house from Chilca, Peru. *American Antiquity* **30**, 137–44.

Drucker, Philip, Robert F. Heizer, Robert J. Squier 1959. *Excavations at La Venta, Tabasco, 1955.* Bureau of American Ethnology, Smithsonian Institution, Bulletin 170. Washington DC: US Government Printing Office.

Elam, J. Michael 1989. Defensible and fortified sites. In *Monte Alban's hinterland,* Part II, Vol. I, Stephen A. Kowalewski, Gary M. Feinman, Laura Finsten, Richard E. Blanton, Linda M. Nicholas, 395–407. Memoirs of the Museum of Anthropology 23. Ann Arbor: University of Michigan.

Fash, William L. 1991. *Scribes, warriors and kings.* London: Thames & Hudson.

Flannery, Kent V. 1968. Archeological systems theory and early Mesoamerica. In *Anthropological Archaeology in the Americas,* Betty J. Meggers (ed.), 67-87. Washington DC: Anthropological Society of Washington.

1973. The origins of agriculture. *Annual Review of Anthropology* **2**, 271–310.

Flannery, Kent V. & Joyce Marcus (eds) 1983. *The Cloud People: divergent evolution of the Zapotec and Mixtec civilizations.* New York: Academic Press.

Folan, William J. 1992. Calakmul, Campeche: a centralized urban administrative center in the northern Petén. *World Archaeology* **24**, 158–68.

Gilman, Antonio 1984. Explaining the Upper Paleolithic Revolution. In *Marxist perspectives in archaeology*, M. Spriggs (ed.), 115–26. Cambridge: Cambridge University Press.

Hastings, Charles M. & Michael E. Moseley 1975. The adobes of Huaca del Sol and Huaca de la Luna. *American Antiquity* 40(2), 196–203.

Haviland, William 1970. Tikal, Guatemala, and Mesoamerican urbanism. *World Archaeology* 2, 186–198.

Isbell, William H. & Gordon F. McEwan (eds) 1991. *Huari administrative structure: prehistoric monumental architecture and state government*. Washington DC: Dumbarton Oaks Research Library and Collection.

Kohl, Phil 1984. Force, history, and the evolutionist paradigm. In *Marxist perspectives in archaeology*, M. Spriggs (ed.), 127–34. Cambridge: Cambridge University Press,

Lanning, Edward P. 1967a. *Peru before the Incas*. Englewood Cliffs, New Jersey: Prentice-Hall.

1967b *Preceramic archaeology of the Ancon–Chillon region, central coast of Peru*. Report to the National Science Foundation (USA), mimeo.

Lumbreras, Luis G. 1974. Sobre los origenes del estado y las clases sociales. In *La arqueología como ciencia social*, Luis G. Lumbreras (ed.), 211–40. Lima: Ediciones Histar.

Lumbreras, Luis G. & Hernan Amat 1965–6. Informe preliminar sobre las galerías interiores de Chavín (primera temporada de trabajos). *Revista del Museo Nacional* 34, 143–97. Lima, Peru.

MacNeish, Richard S. 1964. Ancient Mesoamerican civilization. *Science* 143, 531–7.

MacNeish, Richard S., Robert K. Vierra, Antoinette Nelken-Terner, Rochelle Lurie, Angel García Cook 1983. *Prehistory of the Ayacucho Basin*. Vol. IV: *The preceramic way of life*. Ann Arbor: University of Michigan Press.

McEwan, Gordon F. 1984. *The Middle Horizon in the Valley of Cuzco, Peru: the impact of the Wari occupation of Pikillacta in the Lucre Basin*. PhD dissertation, Department of Anthropology, University of Texas at Austin.

McGuire, Randall 1992. *A Marxist archaeology*. San Diego: Academic Press.

Manzanilla, Linda (ed.) 1988. *Coloquio V. Gordon Childe: estudios sobre las Revoluciones Neolítica y Urbana*. México DF: Universidad Nacional Autónoma de México.

Marcus, Joyce 1976 The origins of Mesoamerican writing. *Annual Review of Anthropology* 5, 35–67.

1992a. Dynamic cycles of Mesoamerican states. *National Geographic Research & Exploration* 8(4), 392–411.

1992b. *Mesoamerican writing systems: propaganda, myth, and history in four ancient civilizations*. Princeton, New Jersey: Princeton University Press.

Millon, Clara H. 1988. A reexamination of the Teotihuacan tassel head-dress insignia. In *Feathered serpents and flowering trees*, Kathleen Berrin (ed.), 114–34. San Francisco: The Fine Arts Museum.

Millon, Rene 1981. Teotihuacan: city, state, and civilization. In *Supplement to the handbook of Middle American Indians*, Vol. I: *Archaeology*, Jeremy A. Sabloff (ed.), 198–243. Austin: University of Texas Press.

Morley, Sylvanus G. & George Brainerd 1956. *The ancient Maya*, 3rd edn. Stanford, California: Stanford University Press.

Moseley, Michael E. 1975. *The maritime foundations of Andean civilization*. Menlo Park, California: Cummings.

Moseley, Michael E. & Kent C. Day (eds) 1982. *Chan Chan: Andean desert city*. Albuquerque: University of New Mexico Press.

Norman, V. Garth 1973. *Izapa sculpture*. Part 1: *Album*. Papers of the New World Archaeological Foundation, 30. Provo, Utah: Brigham Young University.

Quilter, Jeffrey, Bernadino Ojeda E., Deborah M. Pearsall, Daniel H. Sandweiss, John G. Jones, Elizabeth S. Wing 1991. Subsistence economy of El Paraiso, an early Peruvian site. *Science* **251**, 277–83.

Rick, John W. 1980. *Prehistoric hunters of the High Andes*. New York: Academic Press.

Sahlins, Marshall D. 1972. *Stone Age economics*. Chicago: Aldine Press.

Samaniego, Lorenzo, Enrique Vergara, Henning Bischof 1985. New evidence on Cerro Sechin, Casma Valley, Peru. In *Early ceremonial architecture in the Andes*, C. Donnan (ed.), 165–90. Washington DC: Dumbarton Oaks Research Library and Collection.

Stumer, Louis M. 1954. Population centers of the Rimac Valley, Peru. *American Antiquity* **20**(2), 130–48.

Tello, Julio C. 1956. *Arqueología del Valle de Casma*. Lima: Universidad Nacional Mayor de San Marcos.

Thompson, J. Eric S. 1954. *The rise and fall of Maya civilization*. Norman: University of Oklahoma Press.

Trigger, Bruce 1980. *Gordon Childe: revolutions in archaeology*. London: Thames & Hudson.

White, Leslie 1959. *The evolution of culture*. New York: McGraw-Hill.

Discussion
CHAIRED BY STEPHEN SHENNAN

Stoddart: Do you think there is any comparison between the work of Leslie White and that of Gordon Childe?

Flannery: White was different in that White's focus was on energy: White saw evolution in terms of the capture of calories, at the most basic level of all, although to say that is not to do justice to the complexity of his work. What he did was to look at the ethnographic data for living human groups at different levels of social and political complexity and say: "Hunters and gatherers were able to capture so much energy from their environment, whereas rank societies such as Tahiti or Hawaii – and, obviously states with complex irrigation and technology – were at a higher level". So he saw it more in terms of increased levels of energy captured than in terms of any overall scheme, such as the kind of Marxism that Childe thought about. But it is similar in the sense that tremendous emphasis was placed on technological change, which was seen as enabling people to capture ever more energy. Neither of them said, "Well, maybe if you have an ideological or social change, even without a change in technology, it could give chiefs and rulers the possibility of organizing labour and so capturing more energy without technological change".

Rowlands: To continue on that theme, would you say that Julian Steward, Leslie White and others in the materialist tradition within American cultural anthropology represent another kind of reading of Marx, another kind of reading of historical materialism? Perhaps in a complicated, intellectual way we are talking about parallel trends, in which Childe is basically the Old World version and Steward, White and Sahlins, the New World version, and that comparing their different emphases could be a very useful exercise in anthropological history?

Flannery: Certainly, writers such as Marshall Sahlins, and particularly Eric Wolf, have read Marxist reconstructions and philosophers extensively; but the thought of many evolutionists, including possibly Steward, is drawn more from Darwin than from Marx. In other words, we have one set of people who are following Marx and Engels and another group who are saying, "Must there not be a cultural evolution that parallels what Darwin said about biological evolution?" And those two traditions have grown up in parallel ways. There have been periods in the development of American cultural anthropology that were very anti-evolutionary. That has been the major problem for archaeologists: archaeology in the United States has reacted through the ages to what is going on in social anthropology.

Up to about the late 1950s social anthropology was very anti-evolutionary. Then, in 1959, on the 100th anniversary of the publication of Darwin's *Origin of species*, there was a conference on evolution held at the University of Chicago, in which a whole series of anthropologists essentially got up and said, "It is alright to be evolutionary again. We have rejected this for decades, but now it's okay. We just have to make sure that we are not too crudely imitating biological evolution, because we know biological changes are genetic; but we can perhaps recognize different levels of social complexity, and we can use some of the same concepts". During the 1960s, things became very evolutionary, particularly at Columbia and Michigan, and then in the 1970s social anthropology went its own way again – everything became hermeneutic and humanistic, and evolutionists were considered vulgar materialists.

In the 1980s we got sociobiology, coming mainly from biologists rather than anthropologists, although some anthropologists leapt on to the bandwagon. The way sociobiology was originally presented in the United States was *so* deterministic, *so* reductionist, that it immediately engendered a tremendous backlash, so that whatever might be interesting about it was essentially rejected. Now what's happening – and what began to happen, I guess, toward the end of the 1980s, with the publication of books like the Boyd & Richerson volume on dual inheritance – is that biologists and some anthropologists, at least, are trying to find a way of dealing with a kind of "dual inheritance" in which human societies have both a biological and a cultural evolution, with some connection between them, although we don't know what it is, or what effect they have on each other. And we don't have as many articles as we did in the early 1980s saying that everything that humans do, they do to spread their genes more widely. Now the "selfish gene" has met the selfish man.

I don't know what the next stage will be, but there are so many different trends going on right now that you could not characterize all of American anthropology as being in one school. There are people who are absolutely anti-evolutionary, there are people who hate sociobiology, there are people who want to look at some kind of dual inheritance, and there are revivals of interest in cultural evolution which tend to make it a little more sophisticated and a little less deterministic-sounding. And then, one of the most interesting trends of the last couple of years among social anthropologists is that they have suddenly discovered history, after rejecting it for many, many years. What has begun to happen to us lately is that some of our social anthropology colleagues have come rushing up to us, and grabbed us by the lapels, and said, "Did you know that history is important?" This is very satisfying for archaeologists. In fact, some people who work in areas of the world where there has been a lot of archaeology have come up to us and said, "I have just found out that my people have a history that goes back over a hundred years". To some of them we say, "How about trying 1,000 or 5,000 years?" They are not quite ready for that yet.

Gathercole: Professor Flannery, Childe said in a letter to Palme Dutt in the summer of 1938 that he only felt sympathetic to capitalism when he was in the United States, and he had very close relations with a lot of his archaeological and anthropological contemporaries there, as Bill Peace's PhD dissertation (1992) has shown. And Bill has also brought out, in a paper to be published in the proceedings of the Brisbane Childe Conference, the chequered history of the attempt to publish Childe's *History* in the United States after the war. To what extent do you think that McCarthyism and the political atmosphere of the late 1940s and 1950s influenced American academic attitudes to Childe's later work, particularly on the sociology of knowledge and his theoretical stance on social evolution?

Flannery: I don't think there is any question that the McCarthy era had a very deadening effect on American universities in general. It was an era when professors literally turned in other professors as having un-American views. People who worked in Near Eastern and Mediterranean archaeology, however, certainly continued to read Childe, unworried by that kind of thing. I think, in terms of Childe having really widespread influence, part of the problem is that so many archaeologists who work in North America either work on hunters and gatherers or on societies that never moved beyond egalitarian villages, and these are the kinds of societies that Childe was not as interested in and did not write much about. Therefore, their tendency was to read the ethnographic literature on societies of that level of complexity rather than to read him. Since there weren't really any urban civilizations in North America, north of Mexico at least, his writings were unlikely to be as influential as they were among people working in the Mediterranean and Near Eastern areas. But there is no question that the McCarthy era had a deleterious effect until finally people got so mad that they literally stood up and began fighting back; and once that happened, McCarthyism folded like a house of cards, and McCarthy himself was completely discredited.

Harris: Kent, one thing I notice is that you didn't refer, in relation to Childe himself and also the New World view of Childe, to the much discussed variable of population change or population increase in relation to the various evolutionary levels or stages? I would like to ask how that variable is seen by those of you who are actually doing the archaeology on site, particularly those working in Peru. And, more particularly, you mention that Childe's minimum urban population size of 7,000 would more appropriately be 5,000 in Nuclear America. What is the rationale of that statement?

Flannery: I am thinking there of population reconstructions from Mesoamerica and the United States; for most of Peru, we really don't have the kinds of surveys that we have in Mesoamerica, which include population reconstructions. If I had talked more about Mesoamerica, I would have mentioned Bill Sanders, for example, who champions the notion that population growth (and population pressure) is the engine of prehistory, and that it causes changes to successively higher levels of socio-economic organization. Many of us are wary about that because, if you look at biological evolution, population growth is taken as evidence that a favourable evolutionary advance has already taken place, which makes the population grow. I know of no explanation for the appearance of a new species that argues, "It arose because ancestors became too numerous". We are also wary of it in view of studies which suggest that perhaps the state may sometimes have formed at times when the population was actually declining, and not after some enormous growth of population. There is one school, centred particularly in Pennsylvania State University, that does hold that population growth and population pressure are a major driving force, but then there are other people who simply don't want to embrace that view wholeheartedly and who think that, although population is an important factor, it is not the main driving engine of history.

The other problem is that we have nagging doubts about our ability actually to reconstruct real population figures from archaeological data. In other words, to what extent do shards lying on the surface of the ground over *x* number of hectares really translate into 1,000 people, 2,000 people, or 5,000 people, and so on? What Sanders has done is that he has got Spanish Colonial census figures for towns in the Basin of Mexico – we know what the population was in AD 1550 or thereabouts – and he has gone there, he has surveyed the site, he has found out how big it is, and he then says, "I will use this as my conversion factor for shards gathered on the surface to population". The problem with that is that the density at which people live on sites is different at every stage. In the early villages we studied in Mexico, on one hectare of land we know from excavation that we have houses that could not have held more than 3, 4, or maybe 5 people, spaced 20 to 40 metres apart, so that there may have been no more than 10 households spaced on a hectare – that's an estimate of perhaps 50 people per hectare. In later periods, we know that people are living in large, mud-walled, residential compounds and there are many, many more people, possibly 100 or 200 people per hectare; and then for some of the urban centres it may be even higher than that. So, to use only one conversion factor for the whole of a prehistoric sequence seems to us stretching it a bit. No-one has yet come up with (methodologically, at least) a really convincing formula for converting what you see on the surface when you do a settlement-pattern survey to sheer population size. What they have done is to say, "I have surveyed the valley; I think the population size was 16,500. My calculations are that the amount of land in the valley could provide maize fields for so many people, therefore there is population pressure". That procedure breaks down the minute that you find out that the conversion factor – turning hectares of occupied area into people – may be wrong.

Shennan: May I interject a supplementary to David's question in relation to population? In recent years the classic model of chiefdoms has been based on population in relation to circumscription and you talk about the rise of Peruvian chiefdoms in relation to warfare. Well, why does the warfare develop? Is this also to do with a circumscription model with or without population growth?

Flannery: Well, for many of us, chiefdoms and the Peruvian case are problematic because we don't have as many settlement-pattern surveys as we do for some areas of Mesoamerica. Some people now would see it not in terms of land per se, but would look at the demographic factor as an attempt to recruit manpower. Therefore, the crucial variable may not be, as Sanders thinks it is, land and water, but the desire of each chief to bring as many people under his control as possible without being concerned about whether they are fishers, farmers or whatever. What the chief may be doing is taking people away from rival chiefs, who live in other areas. Certainly, some people, such as Carneiro, see it in terms of "Here's a valley, here's the area that could be irrigated, and here's a mountain range on either side. You can only expand so much before you're circumscribed by the mountain ranges, or by another group". But you can also see it in terms of a chieftain becoming powerful and, let's say, recalling that the chief in the next valley controls 1500 people whom he would like to have, and thinking that he can literally take that area away from his rival. That process might happen before the absolute limits (in terms of how many people the food grown in the valley could support) are reached. So, certainly, there is one group who believe that circumscription and population growth have something to do with it. Others, looking at the ethnographic record, sometimes see evidence of a chief moving in on his rival in the next valley long before food would become a limiting factor, just because he wants to have even more craftsmen making even more goods for him. There are such cases, where you can see the move being made long before the theoretical agricultural limits in the valley are reached. So that is something about which debate will rage, probably for many decades.

Trigger: You have really raised an important point, I think, about Childe's attitude to warfare. Over and over again, Childe says in his writings that war is bad because it destroys wealth. Similarly, he regards religion as bad and he fears it because it is powerful. But I detect another blind spot. You said that Childe was interested in technology and I think that's right, but there is a letter that he wrote to Crawford (on 3 January 1941), while he was writing *What happened in history*, which struck me personally very strongly because I knew the person mentioned in it.

The letter said two things: one, that *What happened in history* was going to go up to the dawn of capitalism, and, secondly, that "I really don't know anything about ancient economics. Everything that I am definite about, I am getting out of Fritz Heichelheim's *Wirtschaftsgeschichte des Altertums*" (which has since been translated into English, but at that time was available only in German). Heichelheim was a refugee from Germany who was at this period at Cambridge but who came later to the University of Toronto, where he died, I think, in the 1960s. But, two things are very clear: one is that Heichelheim was an extremely right-wing individual – not right-wing in the sense of being pro-Nazi, but right-wing in the sense of being politically conservative. So, I think one has to add economics to Childe's blind spots. And, as someone who knew Heichelheim, it has always concerned me that here was someone who had published in German – a classicist although he wrote about ancient Egypt and Mesopotamia – who really needed recognition because he was a refugee without a secure job (he had some sort of fellowship at Cambridge). So I have always been worried about that omission – it was another of Childe's blind spots.

Wright: I wonder if you think that, if Childe were alive today, he would be forced to add warfare to his criteria on the basis of the Near Eastern data alone? In your lecture you said that it is more difficult to identify early rank societies in the Near East than in the New World. I agree, but I find it interesting that, when it does appear in the Near East fairly unambiguously, it is associated with burned monumental buildings, as at Choga Mish, and with the foundation of Susa. So, I wonder if you would care to speculate whether, if Childe had had the Near Eastern data that are now available, he would have revised his view?

Flannery: I do not want to get too far into the psychology of someone I never met. Since I never met him, it is hard to imagine what he would think. I would guess that, as time goes on, it will be harder and harder to ignore the notion that warfare is not just a destroyer but also a creator of states; and it may simply be that his moral and ethical values were such that that was not something he wanted to consider as a possibility, preferring to think that warfare can only destroy things. I don't know how he would have dealt with it, but I think you are right that, given the body of data we have now, he probably would have had at least to mention it. He could not just pretend that all of this was happening because the surplus was getting bigger.

Okamura: I believe that processual archaeologists sometimes recognize processual aspects in Childe's late works. Could you answer on that point?

Flannery: On tendencies towards processualism?

Okamura: Yes. Sometimes Western processual archaeologists regard his late work as also an earlier stage of processual archaeology. Is that a misunderstanding?

Flannery: I suppose it depends on your definition of what is processual. Processual, in terms of, let's say, how it was seen in the 1960s, does not come out of social theory, or Childe – it comes out of the ecological work that was being done in the 1960s, in which people began to use simulation models in conjunction with ecological data.

But let me answer in a different way. There is a great tendency for people – not only archaeologists and social scientists, but people in general – to think that two things are connected if they are close together in time and space. What the long-term simulations that people were developing in wildlife management and herd ecology in the 1960s found out was that this is not necessarily the case, and that frequently cause and effect in long-term ecological systems are very widely separated in time and space. What the simulations began to show is that when something happens way back in time A, it may have no effect for a long period but then, in time B, it may cause an effect. So in order to find out what caused these two changes, you can't look at them and say, "Well, x and y happened very closely together in time and space, therefore either x is the cause of y, or y is the cause of x", which is what so often happened in archaeology. What you have to say is, "x and y are coincident symptoms of something that happened far, far back in time". Now, archaeologists feel that they are uniquely suited to studying long-term processes in a way that other social scientists are not; that because they deal with long sequences of changes happening over thousands of years they are in a better position than, let's say, ethnologists or sociologists to see what the long-term and much delayed effects may be of something that happened far back in time. For example, we think maybe that we can see in the archaeological record something happening in 1500 or 1000 BC which might not have a significant effect until AD 500 or 1000.

The way that processual archaeology was originally conceived of, by the people that I knew and worked with in the 1960s, was not some kind of monolithic environmental determinism that ruled out religion and various ideologies. It was an attempt to focus on processes rather than events – not to say, "This happened because a particular decision was made at this moment", but to examine what the long-term consequences of a seemingly innocent-looking change or decision far back in time may have been. And we saw in the ecological literature people doing this with long-term simulations in which they were able to take several processes and let them run for what would be the equivalent of hundreds or even thousands of years, to see if – cumulatively over time – they would have a major effect that could not possibly have been recognized at the time the decision was made, or the change took place. There was never any sense – at least among the people that I worked with – that we were looking at how the environment or the economy was able to cause certain changes. We were perfectly willing to hypothesize that an ideological change far back in time might cause some major economic change much later on. We never thought that there was any aspect of human behaviour that should be excluded from analysis.

I don't see that kind of processual archaeology in Childe or even necessarily in Julian Steward, who would be saying, "Here is the environment that these Indians lived in, so they had to live in it in a certain way". Steward did not say, "Let's go back 5,000 years before the present and ask ourselves what decision the Indians might have made that would have led to them being as they were when first seen by Europeans". I don't know whether I could see my version of processual archaeology in anything that Childe wrote. It is possible that if I searched for it, I might find some parallels in his work; but what we were all looking at was people doing ecological studies, who were trying to show that seemingly insignificant behavioural changes can have enormous long-term consequences, and that you can't always identify cause and effect by seeing them close together in time and space. In the case of some long-term and very important systemic changes, the cause may lie so far back in time, or so far away in space, that simple correlation of that type would not discover their actual relationship.

Shennan: One of the things that I have always thought about Professor Flannery's career was that it was distinguished not only by a strong insistence on the importance of actually doing field archaeology but of doing it with a theoretically informed perspective. He has combined that today with his enormous range of knowledge of Old World and New World civilizations to give us an extremely interesting American perspective on Childe's contribution.

References

Boyd, R. & P. J. Richerson. 1985. *Culture and the evolutionary process.* Chicago: University of Chicago Press.

Heichelheim, F. M. 1938 *Wirtschaftsgeschichte des Altertums, vom Paläolithikum bis zur Völkerwanderung der Germanen, Slaven und Araber* [2 vols]. Leiden: A. W. Sijthoff.

Peace, W., in press. V. Gordon Childe and the Cold War. In *Childe and Australia: archaeology, politics and ideas*, T. Irving, G. Melleuish, P. Gathercole (eds). Brisbane; University of Queensland Press.

Peace, W. 1992. *The enigmatic career of Vere Gordon Childe.* PhD dissertation, Department of Anthropology, Columbia University, New York.

Concluding remarks
Childe and the study of culture process

COLIN RENFREW

It has been a rewarding experience to participate in this Centenary Conference. To offer "concluding remarks" is no easy task, since many of the things
which one might have said have been expressed more eloquently in earlier
papers. After thanking the Director and the organizers for inviting us to this
very appropriate celebration of Gordon Childe, I would like to say what a
great pleasure it has been to hear the long-delayed first paper in Britain of
Professor Leo Klejn, who was to have participated in the Sheffield Conference
of 1971, had political circumstances then permitted.

Although inevitably most of the papers have come from scholars who did
not know Childe personally, it was particularly interesting to hear of Childe's
early days in Australia from John Mulvaney, who came to know him on his
final return there. The informal contributions after the Conference Dinner
were also informative on the sometimes elusive personal side of Childe's life.
Sinclair Hood eloquently emphasized the integrity of Childe, and Nancy
Sandars the courtesy and sympathy with which he ran his personal and academic dealings with his students. The contribution by Howard Kilbride-Jones
(Postscript, this volume) was particularly illuminating, testifying to his
shyness, yet at the same time to a kind of flamboyance. This could lead one
to suspect that there might sometimes be an element of tongue-in-cheek in
some of his more obvious expressions of Marxist adherence: on insisting upon
reading the *Daily Worker* at the Athenaeum for instance.

There is, of course, no doubt that Childe was a committed Marxist, but
even with the hindsight of several decades he remains a difficult man to
understand, from the political standpoint. Peter Gathercole mentioned to us
that he encountered Childe wearing a black tie of mourning, following the
death of Stalin. Yet it is difficult to imagine that Childe did not have some
inkling of the true character of Stalin, one of the great monsters of our time
and of all time. So there was flamboyance, but also some blinkering. The
contrast is difficult to analyze, and will remain, I think, one of the many
paradoxes of Childe's life and work.

Bruce Trigger's admirable introductory paper developed most of the main
themes which one would wish to cover, and indeed developed them so fully
that to touch on some of them again would be otiose. But I will make one

121

critical comment, which I have already made in private to him. As so often with Trigger's work, I find his perception of the past under study – in this case the life and work of Childe – so much more satisfying than his rapid appraisals of the current state of archaeology, depending, as they sometimes do, upon a rather schematic assessment of contemporary politics. The study of Childe which he offered us is so much more convincing than the rapid overview of the present, with which he concluded his analysis. He accepted, it seemed, the varied critique of processual archaeology, offered by those claiming to practice "post-processual" archaeology, who develop lines of thought which would, in my view, more accurately be designated anti-processual. To offer "post-processual" archaeology, as Trigger has done, as one of the three principal movements in archaeological thought in our century (the others being the traditional culture–historical approach, and the processual approach) seems to do for archaeology very much what Jacques Derrida has done for philosophy.

My aim is, rather, to look at some of Childe's achievements, and to make the point that Childe himself was in several ways a pioneer of processual archaeology. Yet in the end his outlook prevented him from developing his most promising initiatives in that direction and from himself introducing some of the basic concepts of the "new" archaeology (as processual archaeology was initially termed). Trigger touched upon this point very effectively when he pointed out that Childe was not only a master of synthesis: he was something of an innovator also of imaginative case studies. His study of the spatial distribution of chambered tombs on the Orcadian island of Rousay (Childe 1942b) is an excellent case in point: it anticipated in many ways the study of site patterning, the spatial analysis, and the relationship between social and spatial organization which became major growth points in the early years of processual archaeology.

This was a paper which, to a considerable extent, had much that anticipated the "new" archaeology, in the sense that it was a careful although limited case study, and yet one which had – or certainly could have had, if the claim had been made – a very much wider relevance. Childe could have developed seminal case studies such as this, but in fact very rarely used site-specific work to develop more general ideas. His case studies often had a broader brush, although some of them were novel and informative, like his overviews of the early use and significance of the plough, of the wheel, and of the horse.

There is a dilemma here, between Childe as a processual or "new archaeologist", very much heralding the archaeology of the 1960s and 1970s, and Childe as a traditional, historical archaeologist, preferring narrative to analysis. It comes close to the final paradox in Childe's life of many paradoxes.

How did it come about that Britain's leading prehistorian of the time (and Australia's also) – in a sense the world's leading prehistorian – should take his own life? Of course his was not a life of rich nor particularly close friendships, and no doubt he had medical concerns as well as financial ones. But the broader answer relates, I have no doubt, to his very modest self-image, which comes out clearly in his "Retrospect" (1958), and in his posthumously published farewell letter (Childe 1980). Yet when we look at the great repertoire of Childe's achievements, and the directions that they could have taken – and indeed some of them did later lead to further developments – it is extraordinary that he felt that he had nothing more to contribute, and that he lacked the curiosity to sit back and see what happened next.

Childe, after all, had accomplished two massive achievements. First there was the great synthesis of *The dawn of European civilisation* (1925), some of it anticipated perhaps in his preparations for *The Danube in prehistory* (1929), a success repeated in *The most ancient East* (1928), and later in *New light on the most ancient East* (1934). The methodology which he forged for *The dawn*, and made explicit with his definition of the archaeological "culture" in *The Danube*, although in part due to Kossinna, was the basic foundation for the study of European prehistory between the wars. Secondly, there was his development of economic and social themes in prehistory which undoubtedly makes him one of the fathers of processual thought in archaeology. His vision of change in *Man makes himself* (1936) and in *What happened in history* (1942a), along with his concepts of the Neolithic Revolution and the Urban Revolution, may be regarded as the first coherent analysis of the processes of change at work in prehistoric times.

Along with these two achievements there was his enduring interest in what precisely it was that was special to European prehistory, which made Europe such a dynamic centre of change in the Greek and Roman periods. Bruce Trigger in his paper remarked very well that Childe was excessively if characteristically modest in emphasizing, in his "Retrospect", the contribution made in 1940 by Christoper Hawkes's *Prehistoric foundations of Europe* towards the definition of this specially European identity. For Childe himself had already shown the way. And in stressing these contributions we are already overlooking so many more: his work at Skara Brae for instance. Nor should one underestimate his willingness to change his mind and admit when he was wrong. Indeed, it used to annoy his followers and students, who had just mastered, and then proceeded to advocate, his recent arguments, when he would suddenly announce that he had been in error, and take a completely different tack.

In exploring this central theme of Childe as almost, but not quite, a processual archaeologist (in the modern sense), it is worth stressing that his work has been perceived in very different ways on the two sides of the Atlantic. In Britain, Childe was seen as the Great Synthesizer of European and Near Eastern prehistory. Stuart Piggott expressed this well in an amusing verse (Piggott 1958: 77), of which the refrain was: "You'll find it in a footnote to *The dawn*". That was Childe: the greatest particularist who at the same time was able to bring all these details together into the broad, overarching synthesis. It is for that, I think, that he is still recognized in Britain and in Europe.

On the other hand there was Childe the theorist, at a general, indeed almost universal level. For, although Childe was focusing upon the Near East, *Man makes himself* is written in very general terms. Indeed the very title of the book expresses in a wonderfully concise way a whole understanding of the nature of human history. (As an aside, let me add that I have not found it possible to arrive at an equally effective title which would avoid sexist terminology; "Humans make themselves" doesn't really do the job). This vision of Childe's that human reality is something constructed, with social reality a part of it, by the actions of humans, encapsulates very well the whole sweep of human history. The perception that the society and the material culture into which humans are born determines their being, and likewise determines, or at least conditions, future progress, is one that underlines much of the evolutionary archaeology of the post-war period, not least in the United States.

Of course this view is derived in part from the evolutionary thinkers of the 19th century, including Marx. But to bring this general notion into a fruitful relationship with the details of the archaeological record was very much the achievement of Childe.

I was a little amused when Kent Flannery responded in discussion to the question "Was there anything about Childe as an archaeologist which you would recognize as processual?" For while I recognize the validity of part of what Flannery was saying, I had been planning myself to make extensive use of Childe's article "The Urban Revolution" from the *Town Planning Review* (1950b). Instead I will argue, and will draw upon Kent Flannery as my witness, that the processual elements in Childe's work, as admirably exemplified in that paper, remain influential, and indeed today continue to be the most influential part of his work. For there remains this dichotomy in perception: few Americans know anything about *The dawn* or *The Danube*, while European archaeologists esteem these more highly than Childe's more popular works such as *What happened in history* and *Man makes himself*.

Here, as an aside, I would like to make a point about Childe as a Marxist, although (as Trigger implies) it is perhaps more a reflection upon our own perspective than upon Childe's. There is no doubt that Childe, as a Marxist, was able to transcend the over-simple 19th-century evolutionist view by stressing the importance of social context. He was therefore a multi-lineal rather than a uni-lineal evolutionist. But for someone who first came to these works in the 1950s, as I did, it never seemed that in reading Childe's writings one was reading the work of a Marxist author at all. This may well be more revealing about me than it is about Childe. But when I read the posthumous paper "Prehistory and Marxism" (Childe 1979), published in *Antiquity* more than two decades after Childe's death, I couldn't find anything in it which a committed processual thinker would not aspire to – and not all committed thinkers are necessarily committed Marxists.

One reason for this difficulty may have been touched upon by Kent

Flannery in his summary, taken from "The Urban Revolution", of the ten key factors leading towards urbanism. For this very peaceful man did not, it seems, situate change in the past in any clear context of class struggle: that is the element of Marxist teaching so conspicuously lacking from Childe's work. And so it is that, in his own adumbration of the key factors towards urbanism, Flannery had to add an eleventh omitted by Childe: warfare. As a committed pacifist, Childe lacked, it seems, the stomach for conflict which in fact provides the mainspring of change in a Marxian perspective.

The outlook of Childe was, in many ways, close to the functionalism of the early years of the "new" archaeology. Or perhaps one should reverse that, since Childe had chronological priority. Certainly it is easy to read much of Childe's work from the standpoint of a processual archaeologist. I agree too with Kent Flannery that Childe did in many ways in his systematic writing (although not necessarily in his very last theoretical works) undervalue the ideological dimension. Religion was for him, as for many unreconstructed Marxists, an epiphenomenon. Today there is an awareness in processual archaeology that cognitive aspects have to be given a more central place, as Flannery has himself indicated over many years.

In the last analyses, Childe's writings on technology do not depart very far in their ethos from the old adage "What's good for General Motors is good for America": that successful technology successfully applied is what really counts.

The case that I am developing for Childe as an early processual archaeologist can be taken further, and that is what I should like to do before offering the counter arguments – the antithesis – and indicating some factors which ultimately may have prevented his leading the processual movement. A processual archaeologist is, above all, one who is willing to generalize. Against this may be set the preference of the traditional historian (the historiographer, to use the term employed by Trigger (1978)) to deal with specific circumstances and specific antecedent conditions: the traditional historian from this perspective is a particularist. This too has been the position of the so-called "post-processual" archaeologists who have repeatedly argued that to seek to generalize about human affairs violates the independence and freedom of action of the individual: the term "contextual archaeology" has been applied by some of them to the brand of particularism which they advocate. Now there may well be historians (those of the Annales school, for instance, and many Marxist historians) who are willing to generalize, and certainly most processual archaeologists will acknowledge the need to study specific contexts, but generally only in the cause of some more general insight. This dichotomy (nomothetic versus historiographic, in Trigger's terminology) does have a certain validity.

Childe was in many ways a particularist (and I shall argue below that such was ultimately the case). But at times the logic of his analysis led him very close to a generalist position. In *The dawn*, for instance, he wrote about

Europe, but he perceived that, since he was in effect taking a diffusionist view, he could not continue to argue that change came from the Near East without exploring what did indeed happen there. So he wrote his book *The most ancient East*, and shaped a vision of what happened as an "Oriental Prelude". For him, that Prelude really happened in Sumer. For although he repeated several times that he was interested in Egypt and the Indus, and these were the other two potentially autonomous centres of urbanism which he considered, he did not treat them in the same detail. If the Maya were brought in – and this was, I think, the only other early civilization which he included in the discussion – it was somewhat reluctantly, and by the back door. Only in his *Town Planning Review* paper of 1950 does he include the Maya in the discussion, and then only in passing.

Yet the interesting feature of his work is that Childe did reach an understanding, a vision, of what happened in the great transformation process which he called the Urban Revolution. And in this key paper he expressed that vision in altogether general terms, such that his treatment could apply to any transformation to urbanism anywhere in the world. You could, without injustice, term his formulation a model for urbanization, although he certainly did not express it in those terms. In this case he was able to see the phenomenon more widely and express it in a general framework. So that without actually planning to be one, he found himself a generalist writing at an almost universal level. It was perhaps irritating to him that the Maya did not entirely fit the formulation which he achieved, and so, after making a brief appearance, they were not further considered. But if he wanted to, he could have claimed his model as a general one, and gone on to focus upon the differences recognizable in the Central American trajectory of change, just as Kent Flannery undertook with reference to Peru in his paper for this Conference. This would have been interesting.

To substantiate the case argued here that Childe was in some senses a processualist, I should like to quote from his study "Archaeology and anthropology", published in the *Southwestern Journal of Archaeology* in 1946. This may well be one of his few papers written with American archaeology in mind. In a way it anticipates a paper of almost the same title published by Lewis Binford sixteen years later (Binford 1962). As Childe said: "The division adumbrated by Lewis H. Morgan, and refined by Friedrich Engels with his more comprehensive knowledge of European archaeology is still unsurpassed". He continued: "Since 99% of human history is prehistory, and only illiterate societies exist or have existed in sufficient numbers and with sufficient independence to provide the basis for reliable induction, this method offers the brightest prospect for reaching general laws indicative of the direction of historical progress" (Childe 1946: 251). "I suggest that one pre-eminent task for anthropology is just to establish such directional laws or directional tendencies, so that we can determine in what direction culture progresses. . .

What scientific and practically serviceable anthropology ought to aim at is by observation and induction to establish rules showing how several variables change together and affect one another in changing" (ibid., 248).

Now perhaps we should not place too much weight upon these references to general laws and general processes – Marx himself used law-like terminology and relied heavily upon Darwin. But I offer this quotation because it is difficult to find, in the writings of Lewis Binford (if we take him as the most prominent early processual archaeologist), many more references to general laws or to laws of culture process than a few citations of this kind.

In reality, I believe, much nonsense has been written by later philosophical commentators upon the supposedly slavish dependence of the "new" archaeology on the production of laws of culture process. It is true that there were second- or third-generation "new" archaeologists, such as Plog (Fritz & Plog 1970) or Watson, LeBlanc and Redman (1971) who became wholeheartedly nomothetic. So I am not criticizing the distinction drawn by Trigger between the nomothetic and the historiographic. But I am asserting that you can offer almost as many citations of Childe making reference to laws of culture process as you can among the first-line figures of the "new" archaeology such as Lewis Binford or Kent Flannery.

There, I think, the case must rest for Childe as a processualist, a case best established by his *Town Planning Review* article on "The Urban Revolution" (Childe 1950b). It really is as good a general analysis as any written since, in the mainstream of processual archaeology. With his ten interlocking factors, this was close to a systems analysis.

There, in brief, is the perspective wherein Childe might well be regarded as a processualist. But ultimately he was not a "new" archaeologist. This point was well brought out in Trigger's paper, where he indicated those one or two areas where Childe came close to being a pioneer in the field of settlement archaeology. He came close too, in his *Social evolution* (1951) to being one of the great pioneers of cemetery analysis. Such studies, if he had conducted them fully and systematically in the way that many have indeed been conducted since the 1960s, could have had a great resonance, a great impact upon the practice of archaeology, showing the way to more satisfactory methods of analyzing the material. But it was because Childe was ultimately a particularist that he failed to see the general relevance that such site-specific analyses might have in forging a methodology which could be more widely used. And, to use the term most appositely introduced by Mike Rowlands in his paper, it was because Childe was also an essentialist.

At this point it is necessary to turn, and it is not really an aside, to the Indo-European theme. This lies at the nub of Childe's particularism. It is clear, I think, that the Indo-European question was his first great love as a scholar. Indeed I find it immensely significant that by 1922 he had only published a single paper, and that paper was published in 1915, seven years before ("On the date and origin of Minyan ware"). It really is an extraordinary thing that this man, subsequently the most prolific of writers, published only a single paper before the age of 30. *The dawn* came at the age of 33, but there in 1915 he had visited Greece looking for Minyan ware as a possible indicator of the origin of the earliest Greeks. It would be interesting, when John Mulvaney and his Australian colleagues have completed their researches, to have an anthology of Childe's *scripta minora* in local newspapers and other minor outlets, between 1915 and 1922, to see what else he was writing over that period, even if it was mainly of a local political nature. [*Editorial note*. The forthcoming publication of the proceedings of the Childe Conference held in Brisbane in 1990 will throw new light on Childe's activities and political writings in Australia between 1917 and 1921 (Irving et al., in press).]

There can be no doubt that when Childe went to Oxford in 1914 he was much influenced by Myres and also by Arthur Evans, and it may have been at this time that the issue of Greek origins really engaged him. Indeed, I do not doubt that Childe's missing dissertation for his Oxford B.Litt., which apparently cannot be found (Green 1981: 18), covered much of the philological ground which formed the central core of his book *The Aryans* (1926), published a year after *The dawn*, but most of it, I imagine, written long before.

It is often the case that the first articles written by archaeologists, and no doubt by other scholars, are very revealing of their motives and underlying research orientations, and this seems a paradigm case. From Myres he will have learnt many of the basics of a sound, geographical approach as well as a strong curiosity about the archaeological indications for the origins of the Greeks, and the possible relevance of the "Minyans". For Myres's Oxford colleague Forsdyke had written a pioneering paper "The pottery called Minyan ware" (Forsdyke 1914) and Myres himself later went on to write his magnum opus *Who were the Greeks?* (Myres 1930).

From Evans he derived several elements of methodology. Evans's success in using the deep stratigraphy of the tell at Knossos as the basic backbone for Aegean studies was emulated by Childe when he turned his attention to the great Yugoslav site of Vinča (Childe 1927) which in turn provided the starting point for his analysis of Danubian prehistory. Nor should it be forgotten that Evans anticipated Childe in applying to the prehistoric civilization of Crete a term, "Minoan", that was at once an ethonym and a name to designate material culture. Childe himself spoke of the influence upon him of the *Kulturkreis* school of ethnogeography (Childe 1958), but "Minoan" may have been the first archaeological culture name and ethnic name with which he came into contact.

I suggest that this question, the archaeological identification of the first Greeks, led Childe with his powers of synthesis to that larger issue, the archaeological identification of the first Indo-Europeans, and so to his two great early works of synthesis, *The dawn* and *The Danube*. And although he later distanced himself from this Aryan theme, repelled by the misuse of ethnic concepts by the National Socialists in Germany during the Second

World War, Childe's last substantive work on a detailed level in European prehistory, *Prehistoric migrations in Europe* (1950a) returned again to these topics. But his references there to the Indo-Europeans are somewhat desultory; he had given up the "kurgan" hypothesis (subsequently championed by Gimbutas and Mallory), and had, I feel, despaired of finding a clear archaeological solution to the problem of Indo-European origins.

Another and related question is why was Childe not interested in America? Lip-service only was paid to the Maya in "The Urban Revolution", as we have seen. And this touches, I think, on what was almost the unspoken question of this Conference. No-one was so crass as to ask it directly, although it emerged obliquely in the discussion that followed Mulvaney's paper. Why did Childe so completely ignore the Australian Aborigines? John Mulvaney has testified that he did not seem very interested in their material culture, and that impression was reinforced by a comment at the Conference Dinner that there was apparently for a while on informal display in the Institute of Archaeology in London (during Childe's tenure as Director) a photo of an Aboriginal man upon which had been sketched a hat resembling Childe's own. Now on the one hand that was clearly a harmless caricature, making reference to his Australian origin. On the other it does imply that he was not, in the modern sense, fiercely sensitive over Aboriginal rights or dignity in a way that we would expect today. Well, why should he be? He was born a hundred years ago, and I am not seeking to make judgements. The point of my remark is that Childe did genuinely see the social world of the past as Lewis Henry Morgan had described it, as divisible into savagery, barbarism and civilization. Childe was interested in barbarism and in civilization, and not very much in savagery, and thus it was that he went to study in Oxford, and later, after the failure of his Australian political career, returned again to England. It must be that at that time he was turning his back on many things. So that whereas one might have thought that an interest in the indigenes of his homeland would have led him to hunter–gatherer studies, as it leads so many Australians today, and indeed leads so many archaeologists from all over the world to Australia, this was not the case for him. Australian Aborigines were not Europeans and, perhaps for that reason, even when Childe was writing about early hunter–gatherer communities in Europe, he did not make the connection which a processual archaeologist might have made.

Childe was a particularist, I would argue, because he did not really embrace the possibilities for generalization which were offered by his own work. Childe was so concerned with analyzing what was special to Europe, and perhaps to the Greeks, that he did not say to himself, as so many anthropologists would do today, that we are looking at human beings who are born into a specific geographical, historical trajectory, but are all born otherwise very much alike. It is, I think, the whole fun and fascination of anthropology and archaeology to work out why there is such cultural diversity, and to investigate how these very different trajectories come about when the basic input, the actual individuals at birth, are all so very much like each other.

It is certainly true that Childe was a very liberal person. But he was not able to escape from the 19th-century view that there is something fundamentally and essentially different about different ethnic groups. He did not see that human individuals in some sense resemble members of other animal and plant species, and so could be studied using an ecological perspective. For the ecological approach developed, for instance, by Grahame Clark, offers a framework for generalization, and tends to make the assumption that humans in similar environmental and cultural circumstances will behave in broadly similar ways. It was easier, it seems, for Grahame Clark, and much easier for many processual archaeologists subsequently, to take a comparative view and to view what happened in human history as different and alternative trajectories from different starting points and initial conditions, but in which the actors themselves were broadly comparable.

Curiously this was not, I think, part of Childe's vision, even though the splendidly general notions of the Neolithic Revolution and the Urban Revolution have proved so useful in analyzing such trajectories in general terms. For Childe, I think, the real Neolithic Revolution and the real Urban Revolution happened once, in or near the land of Sumer, and the focus of interest subsequently shifted to Europe, culminating in the rise of Greek civilization.

For Childe to see the emergence of urban society as one instance of emerging complexity in the world was not a natural way of thinking. The notion that the formation of atoms and molecules into cells, and of cells into more complex organisms, could be compared with the development of complex human societies would have been alien. The development of the nervous system, the social life of insects, the behaviour of primates – these things which interest us today in seeking to understand the phenomenon of complexity – were not of great interest to him. There is of course no reason why they should have been. He was, as we have been celebrating, born a century ago, and the aim is not to make criticisms. Indeed I began by stressing some of his enormous achievements. My aim is to analyze more fully why he was not really a processual archaeologist, even though, as I hope I have shown, he was one of the fathers of processual archaeology.

Ultimately, when he was looking at the roots of change, Childe never quite grasped the issue (as I see it) as to what was special about Europe and the Europeans. We can no doubt agree with the initial assumption which led him in the first place to the study of European prehistory, that the emergence of Greek civilization – with its literacy, its self-consciousness, its emphasis upon the human dimension, its enunciation of the principles of democracy and its development of early science – was one of the most significant episodes in the human story. But the direction which his researches took, like all those of the first two decades of this century, was to ask what was special about the

Greeks in themselves. A key question was thus to trace the origins of the Greeks. The processual archaeologist, however, would be looking instead at the environmental, material and social conditions, and the trajectory of change, recognizing that ethnicity is not an *a priori* reality, not some essential thing given. It too is constructed, like the other realities of social life, in the process whereby "man makes himself".

To illustrate this dependence upon supposedly innate characteristics, inherent within ethnic groups – what I have here termed "essentialism" – I shall quote first from *The Aryans*, although this is a work which by implication (although I think not explicitly) he repudiated in the light of the later Nazi excesses. There (Childe 1926: 210–11) he writes of: "a people who, whether they were come from South Russia or represented a section of the pre-dolmenic population, were, we believe, Aryan in character. It was these who inspired the higher developments even in the megalithic culture of the North. The interaction of the two types of civilization was the mainspring of a rapid progress."

Now Childe was not a racist: "How precisely did the Aryans achieve this? It was not through the superiority of their material culture. We have rejected the idea that a peculiar genius resided in the conformation of Nordic skulls" (Childe 1926: 1911). In *The Aryans* he found a different solution, although it was not one which he subsequently argued: "the lasting gift bequeathed by the Aryans to the conquered peoples was neither a higher material culture nor a superior physique but . . . a more excellent language and the mentality it generated".

I doubt whether Childe continued to believe that the Indo-European languages were in some sense superior. But at the same time a certain essentialism remained. It seemed in some way to matter which "peoples" were which. Moreover he displayed a preoccupation with a feature mentioned in his paper by Mike Rowlands: hybridization. The notion of the dynamism of inter-ethnic interaction already emerges in the passage quoted above. This can be substantiated by another early quotation, this time from *The Bronze Age*, published in 1930. Here he is talking about developments in Europe in the aftermath of the Beakers:

> Thus three currents met in England during the Early Bronze Age: one from central Europe, represented by the invading Beaker folk, another from the Iberian peninsula, perhaps unconnected with population movements, and a third, plainly mercantile, from Scandinavian countries. That explains the intense vigour and originality of our Bronze Age civilization. (Childe 1930: 167)

Now what precisely explains? It is this strange notion of hybridization, which Rowlands also offered in his paper. In another passage Childe (1930: 159) makes the same point: "Thanks to the blending of two traditions, the native civilization of the British Isles during these two periods was vigorous and original".

That statement was made more than sixty years ago. But I think Childe never completely lost hope that he might find that elusive will o' the wisp, something special and essential, something which was inherent in these peoples and hence something that lent particularity to Europe and in a sense constituted that particularity. Indeed that was, I believe, something important which he sought when he definitively left Australia and emigrated to Europe.

These ideas prevented Childe, I believe, from addressing himself to the general problems of culture change as systematically as he might otherwise have done. Already in *The Bronze Age* we see in his work the first indications of the Marxist re-analysis which would allow Childe to stress social and economic factors instead of ethnic ones. But his generalizations never addressed themselves to the human species as a whole. They were applied by Childe, however wide their potential scope, exclusively to Europe and the Near East.

Most processual archaeologists do indeed believe that generalization is an important goal. It may not be too much to say that the failure to see the way ahead towards such generalizing goals was part of Childe's ultimate disenchantment with himself and with the progress of archaeology. Had he made the conceptual leap towards more general formulations, he would have been a leader, or could have been a leader, of a new wave of thought.

The shortcoming was certainly not his alone. We have seen that up to a point Childe was a processualist because, in some measure, he did indeed generalize. But he was undoubtedly let down by the intellectual milieu in which he worked. For I assume that he received no positive feedback, no reactions of affirmative interest, for his attempts at generalization. He was applauded instead for his detailed factual knowledge: "You'll find it in a footnote to *The dawn*". It is interesting that the valedictory letter that Childe wrote to his Soviet colleagues in a tone of disenchantment (parts of which Leo Klejn read to us, and all of which is published in this volume) contained, as Barbara Bender commented in discussion, not one iota of theory. There is not in it one glimmer of generalization, but instead a series of specific details about excavation methods, catacomb graves and the like.

It is revealing that in his "Retrospect" he deals primarily with the specifics of European prehistory, rather than making claims for the vision set out in *Man makes himself* or for the illuminating general concepts of the Neolithic and Urban Revolutions. Instead he continues to fight out the diffusionist/anti-diffusionist controversy in the theatre of Europe. In sum, I feel that Childe's view of his own work was, in a sense, flawed. It is a tragedy that he did not see how much this work had contributed to, and would contribute to, any conceivable alternative to the story he himself outlined, precisely because the theoretical tools which he had fashioned did indeed have a more general validity.

No doubt he was disconcerted that the chronologies which he had laboured so hard to construct were called into doubt by early radiocarbon dates, and indeed some of them did ultimately collapse. But had he valued more highly his theoretical contributions, he would have seen how much his own work would inevitably contribute to whatever might be built in place of those failed constructs.

It is as a processual archaeologist that Childe's work lives today. The sad thing is that I don't believe he himself felt that, or foresaw it, or understood it, and that he ended his life before it came to be generally understood.

Bibliography

Binford L. R. 1962. Archaeology as anthropology. *American Antiquity* **28**, 217–25.

Childe V. G. 1915. On the date and origin of Minyan ware. *Journal of Hellenic Studies* **35**, 196–207.

1925. *The dawn of European civilization*. London: Kegan Paul, Trench, Trubner.

1926. *The Aryans: a study of Indo-European origins*. London: Kegan Paul, Trench, Trubner.

1927. The Danube thoroughfare and the beginnings of civilization in Europe. *Antiquity* **1**, 79–91.

1928. *The most ancient East: the Oriental prelude to European prehistory*. London: Kegan Paul, Trench, Trubner.

1929. *The Danube in prehistory*. Oxford: Oxford University Press.

1930. *The Bronze Age*. Cambridge: Cambridge University Press.

1934. *New light on the most ancient East: the Oriental prelude to European prehistory*. London: Kegan Paul, Trench, Trubner.

1936. *Man makes himself*. London: Watts.

1942a. What happened in history. Harmondsworth, England: Penguin.

1942b. The chambered cairns of Rousay. *Antiquaries Journal* **22**, 139–42.

1946. Archaeology and anthropology. *Southwestern Journal of Anthropology* **2**, 243–51.

1950a. *Prehistoric migrations in Europe*. Oslo: Instituttet for Sammenlignende Kultur-forskning.

1950b. The urban revolution. *Town Planning Review* **21**, 3–17.

1951. *Social evolution*. London: Watts.

1958. Retrospect. *Antiquity* **32**, 69–74.

1979. Prehistory and Marxism. *Antiquity* **53**, 93–5.

1980. Letter to W. F. Grimes (1957), quoted by G. E. Daniel [editorial]. *Antiquity* **54**, 2–3.

Forsdyke E. J. 1914. The pottery called Minyan ware. *Journal of Hellenic Studies* **34**, 126–56.

Fritz J. M. & F. T. Plog 1970. The nature of archaeological explanation. *American Antiquity* **35**, 405–412.

Green S. 1981. *Prehistorian: a biography of V. Gordon Childe*. Bradford-on-Avon, England: Moonraker Press.

Hawkes, C. F. C. 1940. *The prehistoric foundations of Europe*. London: Methuen.

Irving, T., in press. *Childe and Australia: archaeology, politics and ideas*. Brisbane: University of Queensland Press.

Myres J. L. 1930. *Who were the Greeks?* Berkeley: University of California Press.

Piggott S. 1958. *The dawn*: and an epilogue. *Antiquity* **32**, 75–9.

Trigger B. 1978. *Time and tradition*. Edinburgh: Edinburgh University Press.

Watson P. J., S. A. LeBlanc, C. L. Redman 1971. *Explanation in archaeology, an explicitly scientific approach*. New York: Columbia University Press.

Postscript
Three recollections of Childe the man

Note from the Editor

Most Childe memorabilia reside in the minds of those who knew him, not on the written page. It is therefore worth recording the three recollections that follow, all of which were sent to the present Director of the Institute of Archaeology by former students of Childe who were unable to attend the Conference. The first two are anecdotes, remembered by Emeritus Professor Charles Thomas of Truro, Cornwall (England), and by Dr Frank Mitchell of Drogheda, County Louth (Ireland). The third is a longer pen portrait of Childe, from Howard Kilbride-Jones from St Paul's Bay, Malta, honouring his "one time mentor" and recalling Childe's time in Scotland.

From Professor Charles Thomas, 26 February 1992

I do have numerous first-hand VGC anecdotes. Sample: he used to demonstrate flint-knapping outside the old Institute, in the yard, using large chunks of flint and invariably cutting himself and spattering the gravel with (irregular) flakes and gores. He was persuaded, for these frequent and inept shows, to substitute a large potato and slice it with a knife from the kitchen, and VGC used to buy such potatoes from a Camden Town barrow when walking from Belsize Park in the a.m. The lead-in was "Imagine this is a flint I'm holding in my hand . . . " One day Uncle Gordon forgot to buy his jumbo spud, but this didn't deter him; choking with laughter, we had to stand there while he went through the motions, the opening comment being "Imagine that I'm holding a potato . . . "

and

These 1951–5 anecdotes, bizarre as they now sound, are all factual. The "field trips" to Wiltshire were nightmares, in which the main aim was to avoid having to accept a lift in VGC's awful Hudson Terraplane, with his more than awful driving. It was a trip to Avebury when, coming down the side-road to the Ridgeway transport café for tea and sticky cakes, VGC veered off the tarmac and ran one wheel into a sort of ditch, turned to a much-shaken Ashbee sitting beside him, and said "Sorry, Paul, I thought *you* were driving".

And he really did drink half-pints of rum and cold milk; unless you have

134

ever tried this, you can have no idea of how vile the mixture tastes. On the other hand, my 2 years as a pupil, at a time when he only had about 8 personal pupils, taught me to think in directions and horizons that I would never otherwise have encountered. We were all, actually, very fond of him, and saw a private side of Uncle Gordon (he responded to affection and humour, which he was seldom offered outside) that wasn't apparent from Childe the public figure.

From Dr Frank Mitchell, 8 April 1992

My chief recollection of Gordon is of his appalling driving; he was the second-worst driver I have ever been with, being only exceeded by another archaeologist, van Giffen of the Netherlands.

After a meeting in the Institute – then in Regent's Park – Gordon invited me to dinner in his flat in north London. His car was a vast Ford V-8 coupe, with an enormous boot. When he opened this to put in his brief-case, it seemed to contain a large number of dirty shirts. We set off, and during our relatively short trip not only were our own lives, but also those of several pedestrians, put at severe risk. I can still see a cripple we bore down on making a wild leap for the pavement.

The block of flats where he lived was also remarkable. It was built in liner style, with the passages on the outside, just like the promenades on a ship. But I must say that once safely inside we had a very agreeable and relaxed meal, with much profitable conversation.

From Mr Howard Kilbride-Jones, 6 April 1992

I feel I must begin by congratulating the Institute of Archaeology on constituting this Gordon Childe Centenary Conference to honour the man who set the course for study in the discipline which all of us follow. He was one of the foremost archaeologists of his day, and I speak and write as one of his former students. I would have liked to have paid my respects to his memory in person by reading a paper to this Conference, but old age (I was 85 yesterday, 7 May [this should be 7 March: Ed.]) and ill health (I am recovering from the effects of a stroke) prevent my attendance. I feel too that I should congratulate the speakers at this Conference, not only for honouring Childe with an interesting collection of papers, but for giving of their time and ability to talk about Childe's relevance to present-day teaching, his views and culture processes when, in fact, they never knew the man. I have that advantage, not only of knowing Childe, but he was also my mentor, and for a time I enjoyed favoured student status (I regret if I have lapsed into Marxist terminology!). Therefore I feel that I am in a position to talk about Childe the man himself, with conviction and as one who enjoyed the experience of knowing him; for to know Childe was an experience in itself. Because the cognoscenti at this Conference did not have that advantage, I remain fearful that, in the course of their oracular wranglings, they might lose sight of their man altogether.

Childe would have enjoyed this Conference. He liked people who said nice things about him. It made a pleasant change from what he had to put up with in his lifetime. I have only to mention the race for the Presidency of the Society of Antiquaries as an example of attitudes at the time. Childe's continuing relevance is not only to the 1990s but for all time. He believed that his ideas would revitalize archaeological thought, and he never lost sight of his objective. "A nightmare on the brain of the living?" Acclamation was grudgingly accorded him in his day. He was inordinately proud of being an Australian, in which country his background was impeccable – his father was an Anglican clergyman and his uncle a high court judge; but when he came to Britain, Oxford received him coolly, and, if we can believe our Hawkeseye, remained in fear of his return. He left with a minuscule B. Litt., to which he never once referred. Later he transferred his interests to Cambridge. In Australia, upper-crust society regarded him as being a bit of a drop-out, or another university man gone wrong, as Professor John Mulvaney will tell you – a man fit only for caricature. Yet, this same man, when he came to Britain, not only lent colour to the archaeological world, but stirred it to its depths as well, making enemies in the process. But he was good to his friends, admittedly few in number, but in academe some owe their status to him. He was a bitter enemy, pursuing his opponents to extraordinary lengths. He was difficult to please and he remained critical at all times.

How heavy did Marxism lie on Childe's shoulders? One must see everything in terms of Childe the exhibitionist. There was the wide brimmed black hat, adopted as standard head gear in 1933; the open tourer, its hood permanently stowed away in all weathers, thus exposing the driver to snow, rain and universal comment, and driven to distraction down the wrong side of the road. There was the poster of the nude Australian aborigine, on whose head someone had sketched in outline the wide-brimmed black hat: this poster was stuck on to the wall of the library of the Society of Antiquaries of Scotland and left there for a week – a joke gone a gley, since Childe basked in the publicity it generated. Further publicity was given to Childe by his friend, Donald Mackenzie, who wrote up a daily gossip column in the *Bulletin*, an Edinburgh daily newspaper. *The Scotsman* more soberly reported the details of his excavations and of the papers he read before the Antiquaries.

Childe was not actively concerned about teaching: he was a poor lecturer and he hissed his words between his teeth, and sometimes dribbled in the process. Essentially a shy man, he preferred to lecture in a darkened room, with female students assembled in the front row. He always appeared to have trouble with his primatial jaw. His red button nose became redder with embarrassment at question time. Generally cold-shouldered by his colleagues in Scotland, and because of an unwillingness to accept his credentials, he founded the League of Prehistorians with me as its secretary, to be a vehicle for his views. Subscription five shillings per year. Even the low subscription rate did not encourage people to join the Society, so it folded up after three years. Yet he could be sure of a crowded lecture theatre when he spoke before the Antiquaries of Scotland, perhaps because nobody wanted to miss the opportunity of burying him. I was present at a full turn-out on the night Childe read his paper on his excavations at Skara Brae before the Society of Antiquaries of Scotland. All the heavyweights were present. Childe was in ebullient form. He stage-managed the occasion perfectly. He waited until he had read his paper right through before he came to the matter of date for the pottery; then he announced that it was Neolithic. There was immediate up-roar. Fellows of the Society got to their feet and they shook their order of business papers at him. But the night was his. He had achieved what he had set out to do, and he stood before a howling house, beaming on everybody, to shouts of "Iron Age" from Graham Callander. It was an historic night, for grooved ware had been launched upon the archaeological world; and in the course of time, Childe's detractors had to eat their own words.

Scottish culture pleased Childe, and he took full advantage of it. He kept aloof of political rallys [sic]; nor did he take part in party politics when in Edinburgh. On the other hand, he once boasted that he had read *Das Kapital* in the original German three times. I always had a feeling that Childe's Marx-ism was an umbrella under which he sheltered in order to be different from the rest, meaning of course the Establishment. Agreed, it is clear that Marx-ism clouded much of his writing. He was a great scribbler, staying up late into the night: perhaps he wrote political tracts, I don't know, but I do know that his daytime writing was all archaeological. I also know that when he was in London he joined Palm Dutt [sic] and his circle, and he visited India on several occasions. But his success in being appointed to the chair in Edinburgh secured his entry to the homes of the powerful and the rich, and may have been the cause of his becoming "respectable". He refrained from discussing politics with his students. The opportunity was there to create a "cell" but never taken. Most of his students joined Moral Re-Armament.

By being happy with Scottish culture as he found it, Childe was able to accept the hospitality that was extended to him by Scottish lairds living in their castles and large mansions, many with fine cellars, which many times caused Childe to make a second visit. He counted the premier duke among his acquaintances, and he hoped that some day the duke's private army would provide a guard of honour. He was reticent about these friendships, and great was his pleasure when the Master of Sempil landed his Tiger Moth beside the stone circle at Old Keig. The occasion did the Abercrombie professor a power of good and it was one in the eye for Wheeler, who was on the same publici-ty trail. In the course of this publicity drive, Childe's next move was to trade in his Morris Fourteen for a Hudson Terraplane, a hundred-miles-an-hour open tourer painted white. Everything was painted white, which made a better background for the black hat than did green. Childe drove the Hudson all over Scotland at eighty miles an hour, his poor eyesight causing it to be known eventually as Childe's terror-plane. He liked to share the car with me because I could drive it faster than he could, and Childe adored speed. I can see him now, sitting in the passenger seat, the brim of the black hat driven hard against his face by the force of the wind, a look of complete happiness on his face. We drove from Edinburgh to a lorry-drivers' cafe on the Perth road just north of Stirling, where both of us enjoyed what was then the finest ham and egg breakfast in Scotland.

He could be generous too. Visiting archaeologists had him to thank for the hotel accommodation provided for them in the appropriately named Hotel de Vere, in which Childe lived in two rooms – a bedroom and a sitting room – on the top floor. They came at the rate of a dozen or so a year, men like L. S. B. Leakey, C. A. Nordman and Bosch Gimpera. Parties made up of visiting archaeologists and a favoured student or two were taken to favourite sites, perhaps resembling some of their own, so that they could be evaluated and sometimes measured up, as happened along the shores of Loch Fyne, where I held the tapes while Childe measured up the megaliths.

His favourite food was haggis. When haggis was included on the menu he sent for me, and we shared the haggis between us, to be washed down with the best mountain dew. This sent Childe for the bicarbonate of soda, of which he took large doses, since he had an appalling stomach, badly ulcerated, which he blamed on the privations he suffered from lack of money when he was in London as a young man. Even so, the condition of his stomach did not prevent Childe from indulging in his favourite fare from time to time. He liked Indian curry. When Wheeler came to Edinburgh to give the end-of-term lecture, Childe invited him to dinner at the Indian restaurant in Chambers Street. Both Childe and I had a liberal helping of curry, but Wheeler sat before an empty plate. Litchis followed and again Wheeler shook his head. When I drew Childe's attention to the fact that Wheeler had eaten nothing, he whispered in my ear: "that's because he wears corsets". Later I learned that Wheeler abhorred curry and litchis.

Childe was invariably restless. Within his spare frame there was boundless energy. He led his students up hill and he led them down again into the valleys. Armed with a set of Ordnance maps for the whole of Scotland, he would pick out a site in a remote area, and then he would drive there to assess its importance. Few were prepared to accompany him on these expeditions, so that he invariably travelled alone. It was this same energy which took him over the entire Danube region when he was collecting data for his book *The Danube in prehistory*. Every shard and every vessel described was handled by Childe. The book was hailed as a classic, yet it sold only four hundred copies.

He did not take kindly to critics or to criticism. I committed a grievous crime when I challenged him on his dating of recumbent stone circles and proved my point by excavating the recumbent stone circle of Loanhead of Daviot. He then embarked on a programme of systematic vilification which lasted for some years. Our paths did not cross for thirty years until, quite by accident, we met on the Hill of Tara. There we shook hands and buried the hatchet. I am glad we did, for Childe was on his way to Australia, where he committed suicide. He was becoming forgetful. Childe, who boasted that he forgot nothing, feared that his computer-like mind was about to let him down, and that eventually he would become a burden on the community. In his philosophy, the old and the useless who were burdens on the community should be quickly disposed of. So he took his life.

I like to remember the man who was my mentor until our paths diverged. He instilled in me that deep sense of responsibility which I have towards my chosen discipline. For a man to whom archaeology was everything, he liked others to think the same way as he did. He was a pioneer in that he turned antiquarians into archaeologists. His thoughts were always profound, yet he could be light-hearted about a profound subject, and he was not above ordering a barrel of Somerset cider to be delivered on his excavation at Old Keig, for a bit of light-hearted relief from the air of solemnity which had settled on the site. This is the Childe that I most like to remember.

List of participants

Dr Robert Anderson
Ms Polydora Baker
Ms Joan Barker
Ms Jennifer Barry
Dr Barbara Bender
Dr Robert Bewley
Ms Jane Bigham
Ms Joyce Birch
Prof. Richard Bradley
Dr Jay Butler
Ms Cecelia Capezza
Mr Tristan Carter
Dr Patricia Christie
Prof. Sir Grahame Clark
Mr Peter Clayton
Dr Jill Cook
Dr Harriet Crawford
Dr Pavel Dolukhanov
Mr Eric Dorrington
Dr Peter Drewett
Prof. George Eogan
Prof. John Evans
Mrs Eve Evans
Mr Christopher Evans
Mr Andrew Fairbairn
Mr Robert Fellner
Prof. Kent Flannery
Ms Béatrice Fleury-Ilett
Mrs Eve French
Dr Andrew Garrard
Mr Peter Gathercole
Dr Ian Glover
Mr Adrian Glover

Ms Sally Green
Dr John Greeves
Prof. Anthony Harding
Mr Jan Harding
Prof. David Harris
Mrs Helen Harris
Mr Mark Hassall
Ms Jessica Haynes
Dr Georgina Herrmann
Prof. Charles Higham
Mr Alan Hill
Mr Gordon Hillman
Dr Simon Hillson
Prof. Roy Hodson
Mr Sinclair Hood
Mr David Iguaz
Mr Tadzio Jamiolkowski
Mr David Johnston
Mr Roger Jones
Prof. Martyn Jope
Mrs Margaret Jope
Mr Patrick Killpack
Prof. Leo Klejn
Ms Victoria Larkin
Dr Ellen Macnamara
Dr Charles Maisels
Mr Maitland Muller
Lady Mallowan
Dr Caroline Malone
Dr Joyce Marcus
Dr Sarah Mason
Mrs Rachel Maxwell-Hyslop
Mrs Anne McBurney

Ms Natasha Meader
Ms Joyce Medcalfe
Dr Paul Mellars
Dr John Merkel
Ms Mary Moloney
Ms Dominique de Moulins
Prof. John Mulvaney
Mrs Jean Mulvaney
Dr Timothy Murray
Ms Astrid Naujoks
Prof. John North
Mr Katsuyuki Okamura
Mr Peter Parr
Mr Carl Phillips
Dr David Price
Prof. Colin Renfrew
Prof. Michael Rowlands
Dr Nancy Sandars
Mr Thomas Saunders
Mr Andrew Selkirk
Dr Stephen Shennan
Mr Ian Shepherd
Dr Izumi Shimada
Mrs Melody Shimada
Ms Pamela Smith
Dr Simon Stoddard
Ms Geraldine Talbot
Prof. Bruce Trigger
Ms Karen van Acker
Prof. John Wilkes
Mr Rheinallt Williams
Dr Katherine Wright

Index

Entries in **bold** refer to plate numbers; the plates section is between pages 68 and 69.